AIRMONT SHAKESPEARE CLASSICS SERIES

The
Tragedy of
Julius Caesar

By

William
Shakespeare

AIRMONT PUBLISHING COMPANY, INC.
22 EAST 60TH STREET · NEW YORK 10022

PUBLISHED SIMULTANEOUSLY IN THE DOMINION OF CANADA
BY THE RYERSON PRESS, TORONTO

PRINTED IN THE UNITED STATES OF AMERICA
BY THE COLONIAL PRESS INC., CLINTON, MASSACHUSETTS

PREFACE

For the Airmont series of plays by William Shakespeare, we have chosen a text that we believe more nearly preserves the flavor of the old Shakespearean English than do those of more modernized versions.

In a popular-priced paperback edition, it is almost impossible to include a complete compilation of notes because of the limitations of the format. We suggest that the reader refer to the following excellent textbooks for additional material: *The New Valiorum* (Cambridge and Arden editions); the Globe edition edited by W. G. Clark and W. A. Wright (1866); the Oxford edition edited by W. J. Craig (1891); and the editions by G. L. Kittredge (1936). Also, the following books will be helpful to a better understanding of Shakespeare: M. W. McCallum, *Shakespeare's Roman Plays* (1910); Harley Granville-Barker, *Prefaces to Shakespeare, First Series* (London, 1933); John Palmer, *Political Characters of Shakespeare* (London, 1945); Gerald Sanders, *A Shakespeare Primer* (New York and Toronto, 1945); J. Dover Wilson, *The Essential Shakespeare* (London, 1930; New York, 1932).

Dr. David G. Pitt, who wrote the general introduction for each of the plays, received his B.A. degree from Mt. Allison University in New Brunswick, and his M.A. and his Ph.D. degrees from the University of Toronto. Since 1949, he has been in the English Department at Memorial University of Newfoundland and Professor of English there since 1962. His publications include articles on literary and educational subjects, and editorial work on Shakespeare.

O. H. Rudzik, who wrote the introduction for *Julius Caesar*, was born in Toronto, Canada, received his elementary and secondary education there, and studied English at University College, the University of Toronto. He completed his Master's Degree (on a Wm. Rainey Harper Fellowship) at the University of Chicago, and returned to Toronto for Doctoral Studies (one year on a University of Toronto Open Fellowship, the following year on a Canada Council Pre-Doctoral Fellowship). In 1960-61, he studied at the British Museum in London on a Canada Council award. Since then, he has been lecturing in English at University College, Toronto.

GENERAL INTRODUCTION

William Shakespeare: His Life, Times, and Theatre

HIS LIFE

The world's greatest poet and playwright, often called the greatest Englishman, was born in Stratford-upon-Avon, Warwickshire, in the year 1564. The exact date of his birth is uncertain, but an entry in the *Stratford Parish Register* gives his baptismal date as April 26. Since children were usually baptized two or three days after birth, it is reasonable to assume that he was born on or about April 23—an appropriate day, being the feast of St. George, the patron saint of England.

His father, John Shakespeare, was a glover and dealer in wool and farm products, who had moved to Stratford from Snitterfield, four miles distant, some time before 1552. During his early years in Stratford his business prospered, enabling him to acquire substantial property, including several houses, and to take his place among the more considerable citizens of the town. In 1557 he married Mary, daughter of Robert Arden, a wealthy landowner of Wilmcote, not far from Stratford. Two daughters were born to them before William's birth—Joan, baptized in 1558, and Margaret, baptized in 1562—but both died in infancy. William was thus their third child, though the eldest of those who survived infancy. After him were born Gilbert (1566), another Joan (1569), Anne (1571), Richard (1574), and Edmund (1580).

Very little is positively known (though much is conjectured) about Shakespeare's boyhood and education. We know that for some years after William's birth his father's rise in Stratford society and municipal affairs continued. Many local offices came to him in rapid succession: ale-taster, burgess (a kind of constable), assessor of fines, chamberlain (town treasurer), high bailiff (a kind of magistrate), alderman (town councilor), and chief alderman in 1571. As the son of a man of such eminence in Stratford, Shakespeare undoubtedly attended the local Grammar School. This he was entitled to do free of charge, his father being a town councilor. No records of the school are extant, so that we do not know how good a pupil he was nor what subjects he studied. It is probable that he covered the usual Elizabethan curriculum: an "A B C book," the catechism in Latin and English, Latin grammar, the translation of Latin authors, and perhaps some Greek grammar and translation as well. But family circumstances appear to have curtailed his formal education before it was complete, for shortly before William reached his fourteenth birthday his father's rising fortunes abruptly passed their zenith.

Although we do not know all the facts, it is apparent that about the year 1578, having gone heavily into debt, John Shakespeare lost two large farms inherited by his wife from her father. Thereafter, he was involved in a series of lawsuits, and lost his post on the Stratford town council. Matters got steadily worse for him, until finally in 1586 he was declared a bankrupt. But by this time the future poet-dramatist was already a family man himself.

In 1582, in the midst of his father's legal and financial crises —and perhaps because of them—Shakespeare married Anne, daughter of Richard Hathaway (recently deceased) of the village of Shottery near Stratford. The *Episcopal Register* for the Diocese of Worcester contains their marriage record, dated November 28, 1582; he was then in his eighteenth year and his wife in her twenty-sixth. On May 26 of the following year the *Stratford Parish Register* recorded the baptism of their first child, Susanna; and on February 2, 1585, the baptism of a twin son and daughter named Hamnet and Judith.

These facts are all that are known of Shakespeare's early life. How he supported his family, whether he took up some trade or profession, how long he continued to live in Stratford, we do not know for certain. Tradition and conjecture have bestowed on him many interim occupations between his marriage and his appearance in London in the early fifteen-nineties: printer, dyer, traveling-player, butcher, soldier, apothecary, thief—it reads like a children's augury-rhyme (when buttons or cherry-stones are read to learn one's fate). Perhaps only the last-named "pursuit" requires some explanation. According to several accounts, one of them appearing in the first *Life* of Shakespeare by Nicholas Rowe (1709), Shakespeare fell into bad company some time after his marriage, and on several occasions stole deer from the park of Sir Thomas Lucy, a substantial gentleman of Charlecote, near Stratford. According to Rowe:

> For this he was prosecuted by that gentleman, as he thought somewhat too severely; and in order to revenge that ill-usage, he made a ballad upon him . . . and was obliged to leave his business and family in Warwickshire, for some time, and shelter himself in London.

The story has been repeated in varying forms by most subsequent biographers, but its authenticity is doubted by many who repeat it.

Another much more attractive story, which, however, if true, does not necessarily deny the authenticity of Rowe's, is that Shakespeare during the so-called "lost years" was a schoolmaster. This, indeed, appears to be somewhat better substantiated. John Aubrey, seventeenth-century biographer and antiquary, in his *Brief Lives* (1681) declares that he had learned from a theatrical manager, whose father had known Shakespeare, that the dramatist "had been in his younger years a schoolmaster in the country." This may, then, account, in part at least, for the years between his marriage and his arrival in London about the year 1591. It is interesting to note that in two of his early plays Shakespeare includes a schoolmaster among his characters: Holofernes of *Love's Labour's Lost* and Pinch of *The Comedy of Errors*. But let us hope that neither is intended to be Shakespeare's portrait of himself!

However he may have occupied himself in the interim, we know that by 1592 he was already a budding actor and playwright in London. In that year Robert Greene in his autobiographical pamphlet *A Groatsworth of Wit*, referring to the young actors and menders of old plays who were, it seemed to him, gaining undeserved glory from the labours of their betters (both by acting their plays and by rewriting them), wrote as follows:

> Yes trust them not: for there is an upstart Crow, beautified with our feathers, that with his Tygers heart wrapt in a Players hyde, supposes he is as well able to bombast out blanke verse as the best of you: and being an absolute *Johannes factotum,* is in his owne conceit the onely Shakescene in a countrey.

"Shakescene" is clearly Shakespeare. The phrase "upstart Crow" probably refers to his country origins and his lack of university education. "Beautified with our feathers" probably means that he uses the older playwrights' words for his own aggrandisement either in plays in which he acts or in those he writes himself. "Tygers heart wrapt in a Players hyde" is a parody of a line in III *Henry VI,* one of the earliest plays ascribed to Shakespeare. And the Latin phrase *Johannes factotum,* meaning Jack-of-all-trades, suggests that he was at this time engaged in all sorts of theatrical jobs: actor, poet, playwright, and perhaps manager as well.

Greene died shortly after making this scurrilous attack on the young upstart from Stratford, and so escaped the resentment of those he had insulted. But Henry Chettle, himself a minor dramatist, who had prepared Greene's manuscript for the printer, in his *Kind-Harts Dreame* (1592), apologized to Shakespeare for his share in the offence:

> I am as sory as if the originall fault had beene my fault, because my selfe have seene his demeanor no lesse civill, than he excelent in the qualitie he professes: Besides, divers of worship have reported his uprightness of dealing, which argues honesty, and his facetious grace in writing, that approoues his Art.

Thus, in a very indirect manner and because of an attack upon him by an irascible dying man, we learn that Shakespeare at this time was in fact held in high regard by "divers of worship," that is, by many of high birth, as an upright, honest young man of pleasant manners and manifest skill as actor, poet, and playwright.

Although Shakespeare by 1593 had written, or written parts of, some five or six plays (I, II, and III *Henry VI*, *Richard III*, *The Comedy of Errors*, and perhaps *Titus Andronicus*), it was as a non-dramatic poet that he first appeared in print. *Venus and Adonis* and *The Rape of Lucrece*, long narrative poems, both bearing Shakespeare's name, were published in 1593 and 1594 respectively. But thereafter for the next twenty years he wrote almost nothing but drama. In his early period, 1591 to 1596, in addition to the plays named above, he wrote *Love's Labour's Lost*, *The Taming of the Shrew*, *Two Gentlemen of Verona*, *Romeo and Juliet*, *A Midsummer Night's Dream*, *Richard II*, and *King John*. Then followed his great middle period, 1596 to 1600, during which he wrote both comedies and history-plays: *The Merchant of Venice*, I and II *Henry IV*, *The Merry Wives of Windsor*, *Much Ado about Nothing*, *Henry V*, *Julius Caesar*, *As You Like It*, and *Twelfth Night*. The period of his great tragedies and the so-called "dark comedies" followed (1600-1608): *Hamlet*, *Troilus and Cressida*, *All's Well that Ends Well*, *Measure for Measure*, *Othello*, *King Lear*, *Macbeth*, *Antony and Cleopatra*, *Timon of Athens*, and *Coriolanus*. The last phase of his career as dramatist, 1608 to 1613, sometimes called "the period of the romances," produced *Pericles*, *Prince of Tyre*, *Cymbeline*, *The Winter's Tale*, *The Tempest*, parts of *Henry VIII*, and perhaps parts of *The Two Noble Kinsmen*. Many other plays were ascribed to him, but it is doubtful that he had a hand in any but those we have named. Long before his death in 1616 his name held such magic for the public that merely to print it on the title page of any play assured its popular acclaim. The "upstart Crow" had come a long way since 1592.

He had come a long way too from the economic straits that may well have driven him to London many years before. We know, for example, from the records of tax assessments that by 1596 Shakespeare was already fairly well-to-do. This is further borne out by his purchasing in the following year a substantial house known as New Place and an acre of land in Stratford for £60, a sizable sum in those days. In 1602 he made a further purchase of 107 acres at Stratford for £320, and a cottage and more land behind his estate at New Place.

But his life during this time was not quite unclouded. His only son, Hamnet, died in 1596 at the age of eleven years, his father in 1601, and his mother in 1608. All three were buried in Stratford. More happily he saw, in 1607, the marriage of his daughter Susanna to Dr. John Hall, an eminent physician of Stratford, and, in the following year, the baptism of his granddaughter, Elizabeth Hall.

Shakespeare's retirement to Stratford appears to have been gradual, but by 1613, if not earlier, he seems to have settled there, though he still went up to London occasionally. Of the last months of his life we know little. We do know that in February, 1616, his second daughter, Judith, married Thomas Quiney. We know that on March 25, apparently already ill, Shakespeare revised and signed his will, among other bequests leaving to his wife his "second best bed with the furniture." A month later he was dead, dying on his fifty-second birthday, April 23, 1616. He was buried in the chancel of Holy Trinity Church, Stratford, on April 26.

HIS TIMES

Shakespeare lived during the English Renaissance, that age of transition that links the Mediaeval and the Modern world. Inheriting the rich traditions of the Middle Ages in art, learning, religion, and politics, rediscovering the great legacies of classical culture, the men of the Renaissance went on to new and magnificent achievements in every phase of human endeavour. No other period in history saw such varied and prolific development and expansion. And the reign of Elizabeth I (1558-1603), Shakespeare's age, was the High Renaissance in England.

Development and expansion—these are the watchwords of the age, and they apply to every aspect of life, thought, and activity. The universe grew in immensity as men gradually abandoned the old Ptolemaic view of a finite, earth-centered universe, accepting the enormous intellectual challenge of the illimitable cosmos of Copernicus's theory and Galileo's telescope. The earth enlarged, too, as more of its surface was discovered and charted by explorers following the lead of Columus, Cabot, Magellan, and Vespucci. England itself expanded as explorers and colonizers, such as Frobisher, Davis, Gilbert, Raleigh, Grenville, Drake, and others, carried the English flag into many distant lands and seas; as English trade and commerce expanded with the opening of new markets and new sources of supply; as English sea power grew to protect the trading routes and fend off rivals, particularly Spain, the defeat of whose Invincible Armada in 1588 greatly advanced English national pride at home, and power and prestige abroad.

The world of ideas changed and expanded, too. The rediscovery and reinterpretation of the classics, with their broad and humane view of life, gave a new direction and impetus to secular education. During the Middle Ages theology had dominated education, but now the language, literature, and philosophy of the ancient world, the practical arts of grammar, logic, and rhetoric, and training in morals, manners, and gymnastics assumed the major roles in both school and university—in other words, an education that fitted one for life in the world here and now replaced one that looked rather to the life hereafter. Not that the spiritual culture of man was neglected. Indeed, it took on a new significance, for as life in this world acquired new meaning and value, religion assumed new functions, and new vitality to perform them, as the bond between the Creator and a new kind of creation.

It was, of course, the old creation—man and nature—but it was undergoing great changes. Some of these we have already seen, but the greatest was in man's conception of himself and his place in nature. The Mediaeval view of man was generally not an exalted one. It saw him as more or less depraved, fallen from Grace as a result of Adam's sin; and the things of this world, which was also "fallen," as of little value in terms of his salvation. Natural life was thought of mainly as a preparation for man's entry into Eternity. But Renaissance thought soon began to rehabilitate man, nature, and the things of this life. Without denying man's need for Grace and the value of the means of salvation provided by the Church, men came gradually to accept the idea that there were "goods," values, "innocent delights" to be had in the world here and now, and that God had given them for man to enjoy. Man himself was seen no longer as wholly vile and depraved, incapable even of desiring goodness, but rather as Shakespeare saw him in *Hamlet*:

> What a piece of work is man! how noble in reason! how infinite in faculty! in form and moving how express and admirable! in action how like an angel! in apprehension how like a god! the beauty of the world! the paragon of animals!

And this is the conception of man that permeates Elizabethan thought and literature. It does not mean that man is incorruptible, immune to moral weakness and folly. Shakespeare has his villains, cowards, and fools. But man is none of these by nature; they are distortions of the true form of man. Nature framed him for greatness, endowed him with vast capacities for knowledge, achievement, and delight, and with aspirations that may take him to the stars. "O brave new world, That has such people in 't!"

The chief object of man's aspiring mind is now the natural world, whose "wondrous architecture," says Marlowe's Tamburlaine, our souls strive ceaselessly to comprehend, "Still climbing after knowledge infinite." Hamlet, too, speaks of "this goodly frame, the earth . . . this brave o'erhanging firmament, this majestical roof fretted with golden fire." No longer the ruins of a fallen paradise and the devil's, nature is seen as man's to possess, her beauty and wonder to be sought after and enjoyed, her energies to be controlled and used—as Bacon expressed it, "for the glory of the Creator and the relief of man's estate."

It was, indeed, a very stirring time to be alive in. New vistas were breaking upon the human mind and imagination everywhere. It was a time like spring, when promise, opportunity, challenge and growth appeared where none had been dreamed of before. Perhaps this is why there is so much poetry of springtime in the age of Shakespeare.

HIS THEATRE

There were many theatres, or playhouses, in Shakespeare's

London. The first was built in 1576 by James Burbage and was called the *Theatre*. It was built like an arena, with a movable platform at one end, and had no seats in the pit, but had benches in the galleries that surrounded it. It was built of wood, and cost about £200. Other famous playhouses of Shakespeare's time, for the most part similarly constructed, included the Curtain, the Bull, the Rose, the Swan, the Fortune, and, most famous of them all, the Globe. It was built in 1599 by the sons of James Burbage, and it was here that most of Shakespeare's plays were performed. Since more is known about the Globe than most of the others, I shall use it as the basis of the brief account that follows of the Elizabethan playhouse.

As its name suggests, the Globe was a circular structure (the second Globe, built in 1614 after the first burned down, was octagonal), and was open to the sky, somewhat like a modern football or baseball stadium, though much smaller. It had three tiers of galleries surrounding the central "yard" or pit, and a narrow roof over the top gallery. But most interesting from our viewpoint was the stage—or rather *stages*—which was very different from that of most modern theatres. These have the familiar "picture-frame" stage: a raised platform at one end of the auditorium, framed by curtains and footlights, and viewed only from the front like a picture. Shakespeare's stage was very different.

The main stage, or *apron* as it was called, jutted well out into the pit, and did not extend all the way across from side to side. There was an area on either side for patrons to sit or stand in, so that actors performing on the apron could be viewed from three sides instead of one. In addition there was an inner stage, a narrow rectangular recess let into the wall behind the main stage. When not in use it could be closed by a curtain drawn across in front; when open it could be used for interior scenes, arbor scenes, tomb and anteroom scenes and the like. On either side of this inner stage were doors through which the main stage was entered. Besides the inner and outer stages there were no fewer than four other areas where the action of the play, or parts of it, might be performed. Immediately above the inner stage, and corresponding to it in size and shape, was another room with its front exposed. This was the upper stage, and was used for upstairs scenes, or for storage when not otherwise in use. In front of this was a narrow railed gallery, which could be used for balcony scenes, or ones requiring the walls of a castle or the ramparts of a fortress. On either side of it and on the same level was a window-stage, so-called because it consisted of a small balcony enclosed by windows that opened on hinges. This permitted actors to stand inside and speak from the open windows to others on the main stage below. In all it was a very versatile multiple stage and gave the dramatist and producer much more freedom in staging than most modern theatres afford. It is interesting to note that some of the new theatres today have revived certain of the features of the Elizabethan stage.

Very little in the way of scenery and backdrops was used. The dramatist's words and the imagination of the audience supplied the lack of scenery. No special lighting effects were possible since plays were performed in the daylight that streamed in through the unroofed top of the three-tiered enclosure that was the playhouse. Usually a few standard stage props were on hand: trestles and boards to form a table, benches and chairs, flagons, an altar, artificial trees, weapons, a man's severed head, and a few other items. Costumes were usually elaborate and gorgeous, though no attempt was made to reproduce the dress of the time and place portrayed in the play.

Play production in Shakespeare's time was clearly very different from that of ours, but we need have no doubts about the audience's response to what they saw and heard on stage. They came, they saw, and the dramatist conquered, for they kept coming back for more and more. And despite the opposition that the theatre encountered from Puritans and others, who thought it the instrument of Satan, the theatre in Shakespeare's time flourished as one of the supreme glories of a glorious age.

—DAVID G. PITT
Memorial University of Newfoundland

INTRODUCTION TO
Julius Caesar

Shakespeare's *Julius Caesar* was first published in 1623 in a posthumously collected edition of his plays known as the First Folio; the text in its Folio form is unusually good and presents little difficulty in giving us today what must be at least very close to Shakespeare's original play. This is valuable to know because the play itself is much earlier, its first performance apparently in 1599. There are a number of external witnesses to this date, the most interesting of which is an entry in the journal of a Swiss Traveller who was in London in the autumn of 1599, and saw two plays in London; one of these was "an excellent performance of the tragedy of the first emperor, Julius Caesar, with about fifteen characters." A number of other contemporary allusions allow us to place this play rather exactly in the Shakespeare canon and corroborate what can be found in the play itself, that it stands halfway between a historical study of an important event in western history and a tragedy of destroyed ideals. The play, in other words, links the interests we find in Shakespeare's earlier dramatic studies of kingship (*Henry IV, Henry V, King John*) and his later extended development of tragic individuals such as Hamlet and Macbeth.

To look at Shakespeare's source and its dramatic handling is a convenient way to begin to consider *Julius Caesar*. The source is clear and distinct, almost unusually so when we think of the origins of Shakespeare's other plays. For his three Roman dramas, of which *Julius Caesar* was the first (*Antony and Cleopatra* being in some senses its sequel and the later written *Coriolanus* a prelude to Caesar's world), Shakespeare had access to one of the most popular Elizabethan translations from the classics: Sir Thomas North's translation of Plutarch's *Lives* from a contemporary French translation of the original Greek. Plutarch in the early years of the Roman Empire had written a series of "Parallel Lives" in which he compared eminent Greek statesmen or soldiers to the Romans more contemporary to him; Greece and her history was to stand as a model but also as a warning to the new western empire that had replaced her in the classical world. The significant combination in Plutarch of historical knowledge and moral concern was to serve Shakespeare well. And an added benefit was the gracefulness and charm of North's Elizabethan idiom. In this regard we often find Shakespeare borrowing so directly from North that he would seem to be setting to verse, sentences taken direct from his source. To set these words to verse was of course more than to just chop up North into iambic pentameter, as we shall see, but one does find striking similarities: this passage in the Life of Marcus Brutus:

I dare assure thee, that no enemy hath taken nor shall take Marcus Brutus alive, and I beseech God keep him from that fortune: for wheresoever he be found, alive or dead, he will be found like himself.

becomes in Shakespeare's play:

I dare assure thee that no enemy
Shall ever take alive the noble Brutus.
The gods defend him from so great a shame!
When you do find him, or alive or dead,
He will be found like Brutus, like himself. (v.iv.pp.123-24)

More germane to the play's significance is to discover Shakespeare's more general handling of his source material. For *Julius Caesar* Shakespeare is drawing his substance from three of Plutarch's *Lives*, those of Marcus Brutus, Julius Caesar, and Marcus Antonius. These are three separate accounts of the events leading to and resulting from the assassination of Caesar, three different perspectives or points of view, so to speak. All three accounts are of course in the form of a historical narrative which encompasses many events and a multitude of detail. Shakespeare's most immediate task was obviously to create out of these three overlapping narratives a clear dramatic structure, to endow this history with agents that possess distinct personalities and characters, and to give this history the imaginative resonance of a poem through the qualities of his dramatic verse. These three aspects of Shakespeare's art, then, will have to be considered: the dramatic form and its unity, the development and motivation of character, and the vehicle of his drama, the language and imagery.

THE POLITICAL THEME

Among Shakespeare's earliest plays are his English histories, and *Julius Caesar* can be seen to stand in a direct line of descent from these. It is true that Shakespeare is now dealing with a world remote from him in time and place, but it was a world that was having an increasing influence on Shakespeare's age. The Elizabethan age was a product and a participant in the European Renaissance, and part of this reawakening was an increasing recognition of the presence of the ancient world in modern Europe. Thus the history of the Roman world was in this way also the history of Shakespeare's world.

But in turning to Plutarch, Shakespeare found support for the kind of point of view that he was developing on his own in his English histories. These histories used as their historical material the various annals which preserved in a straightforward way the events of the past. An annalistic framework presented a problem for the dramatist; it gave him a cause and effect sequence but insisted he find his own significance in the succession of events and kings. Shakespeare was to do this increasingly in his interpretation of the English past. But up to the end of these histories the reign of a king is Shakespeare's unit of construction. In *Julius Caesar* there is a new freedom. What Plutarch gave him was the momentous event in which he could center his play, an event crucial not just for Rome but for world history. And he could follow Plutarch's lead by assessing this event, not only in terms of the actions that led up to it and issued from it, but also by being able to draw out the political and moral implications buried in it. What is being suggested is that Shakespeare, out of the three lives which he uses as his raw material, creates two interlocking points of view, one dealing with the political issues of

Caesar's rise and fall, the other developing the significance of Brutus's tragedy.

G. B. Shaw once declared his disappointment with Shakespeare's would-be emperor: "Shakespear who knew weakness so well never knew strength of the Caesarean type. His Caesar is an admitted failure . . . Caesar was not in Shakespear nor in the epoch, now fast waning, which he inaugurated." This is a serious charge, for if it is true, then the nobility of the event and of all those who participate in it, including Brutus, is visibly lowered. But we can consider Caesar's dramatic strength as that of the symbol of an emerging world; to him the others are all related, revealing their political perceptions in their attitudes to him. Brutus's idealism is ultimately inadequate to preserve the past; Cassius, the more practical of the two conspirators, is vitiated on the other hand by his very lack of such a sustained ideal. And from Caesar's death rise the new political masters: Antony, though grief-stricken at Caesar's murder, can convert this sorrow into an advantageous political rhetoric; behind Antony and as yet in his shadow stands the even more coldly efficient Octavius. With him the Empire will come into existence.

In these three men, Caesar and his two protégés, we see the growth of Empire. Julius Caesar himself presents its beginnings. The play opens with his closest rival Pompey eliminated, but the more difficult task still remains, to transform a military supremacy into a political establishment. And in this respect Caesar is not always certain of himself. He is a good enough politician and judge of men (for this is the politician's most necessary asset) to recognize the dangers of Cassius' envy. But he cannot anticipate the fury of Brutus's idealism, nor recognize its treacherous prelude in the winning flatteries of Decius. And he succumbs to the lure of power perhaps too humanly for the thoroughgoing politician. Even Casca can notice his displeasure in having to postpone taking the crown he so dearly wants from Rome. And the Senate's pleas for mercy to an exile drive him to an increasing haughtiness as if, ironically, to give Brutus's fears concrete substance. Caesar at the point of his death *is* a tyrant, as well as Brutus's betrayed friend.

Caesar may die but the spirit of Caesar lives on in deadly form to turn the conspirators' swords ultimately against themselves. It lives in all the major characters and draws from them a revelation of their strengths and weaknesses. Cassius' hot temper boils to the surface as he sees in Caesar's eminence a reflection of his own indignity; it drives him to cunning, conspiracy, the manipulation of friends and to murder. For Brutus the spirit of Caesar is an abstraction he creates for himself that will allow him to murder his friend. He subtly argues himself into accepting murder as a public duty and is only too glad to see Caesar the tyrant and Caesar the man coincide in the Senate. But no degree of ritual blood-letting and Republican enthusiasm can check this spirit. Not only is it an apparition to Brutus at Sardis and Philippi, forcing him to his inevitable death, it embodies itself as well in the political astuteness of Brutus's enemies. Swiftly upon Caesar's death a new Antony is discovered, one who seizes a commanding initiative from the successful conspirators while Caesar's corpse is still bleeding. The very moment of Brutus's success is made hollow by Antony's adroit message; the two parallel funeral orations hammer this fact home. Brutus's defeat is already complete. The only consolation *his* spirit may perhaps eventually have is that Antony, too, will be ultimately replaced by an even more successful imperial candidate. When Octavius utters the last words of the play it is his own glory and his happy day that is rising out of what Brutus originally took to be a necessary murder.

THE PERSONAL TRAGEDY

If Julius Caesar is in this way the unifying political presence of the drama, the equally obvious tragic figure is Brutus. There is a certain necessary parallel method of treating these two central figures, Caesar and Brutus, on Shakespeare's part. Caesar is given a necessary humanity to drive home the brutal fact of murder and treachery even if it mistakenly masquerades as an unwillingly assumed public sacrifice. Brutus, on the other hand, is revealed to be not just a man devoted to his ideals but one who will rationalize his way to murderous action to serve them. If he is a genuine Republican, of which there cannot be any doubt, he is also a doctrinaire one, fanatically committed to any action he sees as necessary and even unattractively sanctimonious if crossed. In his argument with Cassius at Sardis, he does expose a corruption in his partner but holds himself unattractively above dirtying *his* own hands; if he can raise no money by vile means, it means accepting the needed funds from Cassius, who will procure it as he best can. And it must be remembered that it is Brutus's decisions—to show mercy to Antony, and allow Antony to speak (secure as Brutus is in the conviction of his own rightness of conduct), to march to Philippi—that undo the conspirators. Cassius may not fly as high in pursuit of an ideal but he can see the dangers immediately before him.

Making all these allowances, however, Brutus still deserves fully the epitaph Antony can afford to make over his body once he is dead:

> This was the noblest Roman of them all:
> All the conspirators, save only he,
> Did that they did in envy of great Caesar;
> He only, in a general honest thought,
> And common good to all, made one of them.
> His life was gentle; and the elements
> So mixt in him, that Nature might stand up
> And say to all the world, "This was a man!"

Brutus dies still believing that the death of Caesar was necessary, and so it was if Rome was to have been preserved as the ideal that Brutus hoped it to be. His is a death tragic both in a personal and a symbolic way. Driven to adopt vicious means to effect a necessary good, Brutus must overcome his own better nature, only to find his sacrifice a vain one. If he dies holding Caesar's murder to have been necessary, he willingly discovers in his own death the only possible answer to his failure. The tragedy in the destruction of a noble man is in effect the insight Shakespeare gives us into one darkness of human existence. The essential tragedy is in the antithesis between Brutus and the Empire. The Empire as it grows becomes a political reality for Rome; but an equally necessary reality for humanity is the idealism Brutus represents. The two should unite; that they do not is the tragic aspect of each.

Brutus in himself can be seen to contain at least implicitly the tragic tensions that Shakespeare was to illustrate more fully later in the self-destructive qualities of tragic figures such as Hamlet and Macbeth. Consider Brutus's soliloquy as he meditates alone in his garden at night. He cannot possess the single-mindedness that Cassius had revealed in *his* soliloquy in the preceding act. For Cassius it is pretty much a matter of securing his revenge and to do this he must convert Brutus to his cause. But Brutus's meditation itself displays both the crippling hesitancy of a Hamlet and the desperate decision to act of a Macbeth. And yet he realizes all the while the power of the storm raging within him. The tempest in the night and the anticipated turmoil in the state find their proper analogy in the world of Brutus's mind. In this self-divided man:

> The Genius and the mortal instruments
> Are then in council; and the state of man,
> Like to a little kingdom, suffers then
> The nature of an insurrection.

It is in this deepest sense that the tragedy completes itself, not just simply on the political level, but in the witnessing of a man of nobility overthrowing this nobility without ultimately losing it. Dr. Johnson suggested this in answering narrow-minded critics who found Shakespeare's characters insufficiently Roman. For Johnson, Shakespeare's characters were Romans and far more as well—they were striking and profound illustrations of human nature and the terms of its existence.

THE MEDIUM OF POETRY

We have been considering the means by which Shakespeare transforms a historical narrative (or rather three related historical accounts) into a dramatic structure that reveals the

deepest political and moral implications of this crucial event
in world history. It now remains to notice the actual medium
by means of which the conflict and the characters are presented to the audience. This medium is the language Shakespeare uses and the poetry he makes of it. In one elementary
sense the verse is Shakespeare's major convention. The Elizabethan theatre provides several striking contrasts with the
theatre of later ages; at first it seems handicapped in its lack
of scenery, lighting, and all the stage properties that contribute
so heavily to theatrical illusion today. But any such hypo-
thetical shortcomings are more than easily accommodated by
what after all must remain crucial to any dramatic vehicle,
its expressiveness. In Shakespeare this is his language. Place
and time are swiftly and economically suggested in the
speeches themselves; a lighted candle and it is night; a swift
succession of armed men and we have the hurly-burly of
battle. Casca's hysterical fears and descriptive panic drive
home a night of storm far more effectively than any off-stage
noise ever could hope to accomplish. For it must be remembered that mechanical illusions can distract as well as rein-
force the desired effects; by securing the audience's initial
close attention to the language to create the necessary elementary illusions, Shakespeare can then go on to draw even
more significantly upon this attention. It is with this attention
and through the corresponding freedom from mechanical con-
trivance that Shakespeare's drama achieves its fullest richness.
In the poetry of the play characters and events are unified,
deepened, and made memorable.

Consider some of the recurring references in the play to
storm and strife. On the physical level we have Casca's panic
and Cicero's contempt of the violence of the tempest in the
night. But both men go beyond the immediate storm about
them. Cicero rationalistically disregards it in his greater curi-
osity as to what political issues will emerge the next day.
But for Casca the political results are foreshadowed in the
prodigies of the night. Cassius similarly interprets the storm
as an incentive to necessary action. Brutus, as has already
been suggested, makes the same correspondence between un-
rest in men's affairs and turmoil in the skies; but he also

reveals to us a third correspondence, the universe of his mind which also shows confusion and the chaos of conflicting impulses. In his decision to act he hopes to restore calm in the world and in himself. But this calm he can find only and ultimately in his death. Other patterns such as this can be found operating in the play, such as the one, for example, operating on the basis of a pun. Brutus has to show *mettle* in forcing himself to action. The reason he is sought out by the conspirators is that this *mettle* of his, his nobility and ideal- ism, will be a rich *metal* for the conspirators' use. He will give their motives, compounded of envy and spite, a rich appearance:

> O, he sits high in all the people's hearts:
> And that which would appear offence in us,
> His countenance, like richest alchemy,
> Will change to virtue and to worthiness.

Brutus's decisive error is in sparing Antony; and the mis- take is emphasized figuratively: "To you our swords have leaden points, Marc Antony." And one more link in this chain of imagery is forged.

Julius Caesar as a play does not have the full richness of striking phrase and imagery that can be found in some other of Shakespeare's plays, and this is highly in keeping with the grimness of events and the Roman nobility that are the domi- nant effects wanted. How much more striking then is the figure of Brutus when set apart from the other characters of the play by his richness of metaphor and rhetoric. These we find used in strikingly contrasting ways in Brutus, to reveal both his strengths and weaknesses. In his soliloquy as he pre- pares himself for a hateful task, the complexity of imagery corresponds to the tortuous path of his thoughts. But his rhetoric can also be used to inflate his self-justification, at times indicate almost self-satisfaction:

> Set honour in one eye and death i' th' other,
> And I will look on both indifferently.

Similarly, after the murder of Caesar, how much of Brutus's effort to turn the event into ritual and into a rhetorical performance on behalf of Liberty stems from his revulsion to the deed and his wish to justify it.

This, perhaps, should not be pushed too far, for, almost immediately after the republican enthusiasm, we hear a dignified and noble Brutus in the forum, delivering the justice of his cause simply and starkly. It is Antony who provides the rhetorical performance, and it is significant that the persuasiveness of Antony's oration comes not so much from any richness of word and image as from the skillful psychological construction of the speech. Antony depends on structure to lead his audience and saves his rhetoric for private grief where it will not do him any harm.

Caesar is more akin to Brutus in this respect of speech than he is to his successor, Antony. Just as Brutus can be driven to inflate his arguments and to exercise his idealism before an audience, so can Caesar be goaded, too easily for his own good, into a grandiloquence that he considers his due. Notice his response to his wife's fears. He begins with an effective expression of courage, only to build himself up into a lion. At the moment of his death he makes claims to be the Olympian point of order around which the petty Roman world must whirl. If Antony is better guarded in the words he utters than either Brutus or Caesar, he still possesses some depth of grief and its expressiveness. Octavius' few words, however, are sufficient, in their coldness and pompous solemnity, to indicate an even further remove from any richness of speech standing witness to richness of emotion and thought. The "happy day" of Empire that will eventually come will have no room for the swagger of Caesar nor the rhetorical self-assertions of a Brutus; but neither will it make allowance for Antony's richly expressed grief, Caesar's moving words of courage, or the imaginative moral idealism and nobility of a Brutus.

THE TITLE

Shakespeare chose to name his play after Julius Caesar. It is Caesar's death that forms the central event, dramatically, politically, and, most important, morally, in the play; in this significant sense the play is the rise and fall of Julius Caesar. We have seen, however, that the fall of Caesar is, on the deeper level, perhaps essentially the fall of Brutus, for the spirit of Caesar survives. The tragedy we see in Brutus is two-fold: it is his own and it is Rome's. It is a tragedy of ideals that can lead to brutal murder, a murder which does not kill the object of its hate but rather destroys its owner. It is also the tragedy that corresponds to this individual failure in the larger perspective of Rome and world history. Paradoxically, Brutus's act insures the survival of what is hateful to him in an even stronger and more hateful form. Caesar and Brutus both fall but Caesar's Empire rises.

O. H. RUDZIK
Department of English
University College
University of Toronto

STUDY QUESTIONS

ACT I

1. What purpose is served by postponing the introduction of the main characters of the play until the second scene? What essential information as to the immediate historical background is given in the first scene? What of importance is learned about Roman plebeians?

2. Describe the various elements that serve to characterize each of Caesar, Brutus, and Cassius in this first act and the total impression left of each character by the end of the act.

3. Why are some of the speeches in prose and others in verse in the second scene?

4. What do the subordinate roles of Casca and Cicero contribute to the dramatic effect of this act?

5. Discuss the importance and the thematic effect of the storm scene. What are the ways in which Shakespeare conveys the effects of storm without depending on lighting or scenic supports?

6. Outline in detail the steps Cassius takes to involve Brutus in the conspiracy (his speeches to Brutus, to Casca and to the others, his instructions). What do you take to be the major motives for his own role in the plot?

7. Discuss the varieties of humor and comedy occurring in the first act. Do these serve any purpose beyond amusement?

ACT II

1. Analyze in detail the argument Brutus builds up to persuade himself in his opening soliloquy. What are its convincing points and what are its weaknesses?

2. What is Brutus's position among the conspirators? What specific indications are given of this?

3. What are the purposes served (dramatic and thematic) in introducing Portia and Ligarius at the end of the first scene?

4. What further features are added to Caesar's characterization in the second scene to what has been shown earlier? How closely do they agree with what the conspirators have suggested in the previous scene?

5. What purposes do the last two scenes of this act serve? Discuss the importance of the two different points of view as to what is to occur.

6. Discuss the dramatic developments that are sustained and elaborated from the first act. What new elements are introduced and how?

ACT III

1. Examine the details earlier in the play that contribute to give the soothsayer's prophecy its cumulative effect. Why is this effect established?

2. How does Caesar lose our sympathy in the first scene? Why is this necessary?

3. What are the immediate effects of the assassination? What is Brutus's response? What implications does this have for the future of the conspiracy?

4. Examine in detail Antony's message to the conspirators. What does it indicate about Antony's abilities and his probable course of conduct? How is this substantiated in what Antony actually says when he comes before the conspirators?

5. How does Antony gain the initiative from the conspirators? Why does Brutus neglect Cassius' warnings?

6. What dramatic purposes does Antony's soliloquy over Caesar's body serve?

7. Contrast carefully the speeches of Brutus and Antony in the second scene (prose as against verse, imagery, arguments, effect on audience) so as to indicate the speakers' different (a) characters; (b) purposes.

8. Analyze the structure of Antony's speech as a rhetorical performance. What are the steps taken to interest, then win over, and finally arouse his audience? Detail the means Antony uses (a) to discredit the conspirators; (b) to elevate Caesar and arouse feelings of vengeance for him.

9. What does the third scene contribute to the dramatic mood of the play at this point?

10. Where would you locate the turning point in the action of the play? Give specific reasons based on the events, the characterizations, and the language that occur in this act.

ACT IV

1. What new elements are revealed about Antony's character? What emerge as the leading traits of Octavius and Lepidus? In the light of this information, discuss the irony of Brutus's actions and hopes.

2. What new features emerge in the characters of Brutus and Cassius in their quarrel? To what degree can these be considered as the consequences of their act of murder?

3. Discuss the dramatic effects created by Portia's suicide and its reports.

4. What indications are given or suggested that the conspirators are inevitably heading for failure and disaster?

5. Discuss the dramatic structuring of the apparition sequence. What purpose does it serve thematically? How does Shakespeare prevent the apparition from being interpreted as simply a hallucination of Brutus? In what ways is the apparition the "evil spirit" of Brutus?

ACT V

1. What are the two military errors committed by the armies of Brutus and Cassius?

2. Discuss the Elizabethan theatrical convention of the *flyting* in terms of
   (a) its dramatic purposes
   (b) its revelation of character
   (c) its comic effects and the purpose of these.

3. What is indicated about the states of mind of Cassius and Brutus in their farewell speeches to each other in the first scene? How does the fact that Cassius claims to be an Epicurean and Brutus a Stoic contribute to our knowledge of their characters?

4. Discuss in detail the steps by which the battle is lost for Cassius and Brutus. How closely does this correspond

with Brutus's claim that it is the spirit of Julius Caesar
that has defeated them?

5. How does Shakespeare convey the effect of battle and
its course with economy and precision and yet so as to
convey the effect of tumult and confusion? How does
he overcome any mechanical disadvantages (see question five to act one)?

6. What are the contrasts conveyed in the deaths of Cassius
and Brutus? To what purpose? Discuss these two suicides
in terms of climactic progression.

7. Why does Brutus kill himself even more willingly than
he had killed Caesar? Does he ultimately regret or repent
of his assassination of Caesar?

8. What final impression is left with the audience of Brutus
—in his death, and in the epitaphs given him by Antony
and Octavius?

9. What is the final effect of the play? Consider the final
words of Antony and Octavius, adducing what has been
indicated of their relationship at earlier points in the play.
What are the ultimate "glories of this happy day"?

General Questions

1. What is conveyed about the play in its title, *Julius Caesar*?
Though Caesar is murdered halfway through the play,
how does his presence continue to be felt? To what extent does Caesar provide the play with its meaning and
unity?

2. Discuss the varieties of the supernatural in the play, its
differing effect and the over-all impression it gives to the
atmosphere and the theme of the drama.

3. What aspects of the play can be considered political or
public and which ones personal or private? How do they
interact and produce a unified impression?

4. To what extent is *Julius Caesar* a history? a tragedy?
Consider the historical background of the play, its dramatic structure, and the roles and characters of Caesar,
Antony, Brutus, and Cassius. Discuss the presence of a
historical or political hero and of a tragic hero in the
drama and how the two are interrelated.

5. Discuss some of the dominant imagery of the play. Which

images occur repetitively enough to form a pattern and what is the contribution of such a pattern to

   (a) the dramatic action
   (b) the characterization
   (c) the mood of the play
   (d) the theme of the play?

6. From the structure and action of the drama, what emerge as the major differences of the Elizabethan theatre from the twentieth-century theatre? Consider the use of space (locale, setting) and time (duration of scenes and acts, succession of dramatic events and actions), and any other conventions illustrated in the play.

7. Discuss the use of verse as a vehicle for dramatic action and characterization. Consider the imagery used, the contrasting effect from prose passages in the play, the effect of intensity and formality achieved through the poetry.

8. Identify the speaker and occasion in each of the following passages. Discuss its meaning and its importance in the dramatic action and what it indicates about the character of the speaker:

   (a) Men at some time are masters of their fates:
       The fault, dear Brutus, is not in our stars,
       But in ourselves, that we are underlings.

   (b) Cowards die many times before their deaths;
       The valiant never taste of death but once.

   (c) Between the acting of a dreadful thing
       And the first motion, all the interim is
       Like a phantasma, or a hideous dream.

   (d) And Caesar's spirit, ranging for revenge,
       With Ate by his side come hot from hell,
       Shall in these confines with a monarch's voice
       Cry havoc and let slip the dogs of war . . .

   (e) O Julius Caesar, thou art mighty yet!
       Thy spirit walks abroad, and turns our swords
       In our own proper entrails.

   (f) According to his virtue let us use him,
       With all respect and rites of burial.

   (g) I could be well moved, if I were as you;
       If I could pray to move, prayers would move me;
       But I am constant as the northern star . . .

JULIUS CAESAR

DRAMATIS PERSONAE

JULIUS CAESAR.

OCTAVIUS CAESAR,
MARCUS ANTONIUS,
M. AEMILIUS LEPIDUS, } *triumvirs after the death of Julius Cæsar.*

CICERO,
PUBLIUS, } *senators.*
POPILIUS LENA,

MARCUS BRUTUS,
CASSIUS,
CASCA,
TREBONIUS,
LIGARIUS, } *conspirators against Julius Cæsar.*
DECIUS BRUTUS,
METELLUS CIMBER,
CINNA,

FLAVIUS *and* MARULLUS, *tribunes.*

ARTEMIDORUS, *a sophist of Cnidos.*

A SOOTHSAYER.

CINNA, *a poet.*

ANOTHER POET.

LUCILIUS,
TITINIUS,
MESSALA, } *friends to Brutus and Cassius.*
YOUNG CATO,
VOLUMNIUS,

VARRO,
CLITUS,
CLAUDIUS,
STRATO, } *servants to Brutus.*
LUCIUS,
DARDANIUS,

PINDARUS, *servant to Cassius.*

CALPHURNIA, *wife to Cæsar.*

PORTIA, *wife to* BRUTUS.

SENATORS, CITIZENS, GUARDS, ATTENDANTS, &c.

SCENE—*During a great part of the play at Rome; afterwards near Sardis, and near Philippi.*

Julius Caesar

ACT I

ACT I

CAESAR has just returned to Rome to celebrate a triumph for his victory in a civil war against Pompey. The populace uses the occasion as a holiday but is reproved by the two tribunes for their irresponsibility and quick forgetting of Pompey, their recent hero. Caesar is now the hero and conqueror, fawned on by Casca and attended to by the young and quick-spirited Antony at the celebrations of the Roman festival of Lupercal. But this ever-increasing eminence of Caesar's position brings out bitter envy in Cassius, unwilling to have himself held lower than the new "Colossus"; Cassius had once bested Caesar in a wager to swim the Tiber fully armed, even rescuing him during the contest; he has seen Caesar feverish and parched by disease. Why should then Caesar's name have such magic in it? To insure the success of his scheme to bring Caesar low, Cassius approaches Brutus, a man of high principle and renowned reputation. Cassius' insinuations of possible dangers to the Republic from any one man holding unquestioned dominance in it are reinforced by Casca's ill-humored report of how unwilling Caesar appeared to have to refuse three times the crown offered him by the enthusiastic populace. Caesar comments to Antony on Cassius' dangerous appearance; his personal grudges are to be seen in his predatory looks. But Antony discounts the trouble signs; Brutus takes them for public zeal and begins to mull over Cassius' accusations that Caesar is ambitious for a throne. That night a fearful storm erupts; prodigies and marvels seem to foretoken a time of turmoil. The tempest terrifies Casca completely; Cicero ignores it and is more intent on what tomorrow will show at the Senate. The wily Cassius persuades Casca to use the storm as a spur to necessary action, to rid Rome of its monster. A preliminary meeting of the conspirators is quickly held. Cassius issues instructions to have Brutus's involvement in the affair increased by anonymous messages urging him on; the conspirators move to win over Brutus before the night is done.

ACT I. Scene I.

Rome. A street.

Enter FLAVIUS, MARULLUS, *and certain* COMMONERS
over the stage.

FLAVIUS.

Hence! home, you idle creatures, get you home:
Is this a holiday? what! know you not,
Being mechanical,[1] you ought not walk
Upon a labouring day without the sign
Of your profession?—Speak, what trade art thou?

FIRST CITIZEN.

Why, sir, a carpenter.

MARULLUS.

Where is thy leather apron and thy rule?
What dost thou with thy best apparel on?—
You, sir, what trade are you?

SECOND CITIZEN.

Truly, sir, in respect of[2] a fine workman, I am but,
as you would say, a cobbler.[3]

MARULLUS.

But what trade art thou? answer me directly.

SECOND CITIZEN.

A trade, sir, that I hope I may use with a safe conscience;
which is, indeed, sir, a mender of bad soles.

MARULLUS.

What trade, thou knave? thou naughty knave, what trade?

---

[1] mechanical: artisans; workers.
[2] in respect of: in comparison with.
[3] cobbler: one that does clumsy work; a botcher.

SECOND CITIZEN.

Nay, I beseech you, sir, be not out with me: yet if you be
out, sir, I can mend you.

MARULLUS.

What meanest thou by that? mend me, thou saucy fellow!

SECOND CITIZEN.

Why, sir, cobble you.

FLAVIUS.

Thou art a cobbler, art thou?

SECOND CITIZEN.

Truly, sir, all that I live by is with the awl:[1] I meddle with
no tradesman's matters, nor women's matters, but with awl.
I am, indeed, sir, a surgeon to old shoes; when they are in
great danger, I recover them. As proper men[2] as ever trod
upon neats-leather[3] have gone upon[4] my handiwork.

FLAVIUS.

But wherefore art not in thy shop to-day?
Why dost thou lead these men about the streets?

SECOND CITIZEN.

Truly, sir, to wear out their shoes, to get myself into more
work. But, indeed, sir, we make holiday, to see Cæsar, and
to rejoice in his triumph.

MARULLUS.

Wherefore rejoice? What conquest brings he home?
What tributaries follow him to Rome,
To grace in captive bonds his chariot-wheels?
You blocks,[5] you stones, you worse than senseless things!
O you hard hearts, you cruel men of Rome,

---

[1] awl: a piercing tool used in leather work.
[2] proper men: good men; respectable men.
[3] neats-leather: cowhide.
[4] gone upon: walked on.
[5] blocks: unfeeling and stupid persons.

Knew you not Pompey? Many a time and oft
Have you climb'd up to walls and battlements,
To towers and windows, yea, to chimney-tops,
Your infants in your arms, and there have sat
The live-long day, with patient expectation,
To see great Pompey pass the streets of Rome:
And when you saw his chariot but appear,
Have you not made an universal shout,
That Tiber[1] trembled underneath her banks,
To hear the replication[2] of your sounds
Made in her concave shores?
And do you now put on your best attire?
And do you now cull out[3] a holiday?
And do you now strew flowers in his way
That comes in triumph over Pompey's blood?
Be gone!
Run to your houses, fall upon your knees,
Pray to the gods to intermit[4] the plague
That needs must light on this ingratitude.

    FLAVIUS.

Go, go, good countrymen, and, for this fault,
Assemble all the poor men of your sort;
Draw them to Tiber banks, and weep your tears
Into the channel, till the lowest stream
Do kiss the most exalted shores of all.[5]

                        [*Exeunt all the* COMMONERS.

See, whe'r their basest metal [6] be not moved!
They vanish tongue-tied in their guiltiness.
Go you down that way towards the Capitol;
This way will I: disrobe the images,
If you do find them deckt with ceremonies.[7]

---

[1] Tiber: a river of Central Italy that cuts through Rome. [2] replication: echo. [3] cull out: select. [4] intermit: discontinue; suspend. [5] kiss the most exalted shores of all: overflow its highest banks. [6] basest metal: lowest nature. [7] ceremonies: symbols used in religious observances.

MARULLUS.

May we do so?
You know it is the feast of Lupercal.[1]

FLAVIUS.

It is no matter; let no images
Be hung with Cæsar's trophies. I'll about,
And drive away the vulgar[2] from the streets:
So do you too, where you perceive them thick.
These growing feathers pluckt from Cæsar's wing
Will make him fly an ordinary pitch;[3]
Who else would soar above the view of men,
And keep us all in servile fearfulness.   [*Exeunt.*

SCENE II.

The same. A public place.

Enter CAESAR; ANTONY, *for the course;* CALPHURNIA, PORTIA,
DECIUS, CICERO, BRUTUS, CASSIUS, & CASCA; *a great crowd
following, among them a* SOOTHSAYER.

JULIUS CAESAR.

Calphurnia,—

CASCA.

        Peace, ho! Cæsar speaks.   [*Music ceases.*

JULIUS CAESAR.

           Calphurnia,—

CALPHURNIA.

Here, my lord.

JULIUS CAESAR.

Stand you directly in Antonius' way,
When he doth run his course.—Antonius,—

MARCUS ANTONIUS.

Cæsar, my lord?

---

[1] the feast of Lupercal: an ancient festival celebrated in February
to insure fertility.
[2] vulgar: lowest class.
[3] pitch: height.

JULIUS CAESAR.

Forget not, in your speed, Antonius,
To touch Calphurnia; for our elders say,
The barren, touched in this holy chase,
Shake off their sterile curse.

MARCUS ANTONIUS.

                    I shall remember:
When Cæsar says 'Do this,' it is perform'd.

JULIUS CAESAR.

Set on; and leave no ceremony out.   [*Music.*

SOOTHSAYER.

Cæsar!

JULIUS CAESAR.

Ha! who calls?

CASCA.

Bid every noise be still:—peace yet again!   [*Music ceases.*

JULIUS CAESAR.

Who is it in the press that calls on me?
I hear a tongue, shriller than all the music,
Cry 'Cæsar.' Speak; Cæsar is turn'd to hear.

SOOTHSAYER.

Beware the ides of March.[1]

JULIUS CAESAR.

                What man is that?

MARCUS BRUTUS.

A soothsayer bids you beware the ides of March.

JULIUS CAESAR.

Set him before me; let me see his face.

CASSIUS.

Fellow, come from the throng; look upon Cæsar.

---

[1] the ides of March: the 15th day of March in the ancient Roman calendar; broadly, this day and the seven days preceding it.

JULIUS CAESAR.

What say'st thou to me now? speak once again.

SOOTHSAYER.

Beware the ides of March.

JULIUS CAESAR.

He is a dreamer; let us leave him:—pass.

              [Sennet. Exeunt all but BRUTUS *and* CASSIUS.

CASSIUS.

Will you go see the order of the course?[1]

MARCUS BRUTUS.

Not I.

CASSIUS.

I pray you, do.

MARCUS BRUTUS.

I am not gamesome: I do lack some part
Of that quick spirit that is in Antony.
Let me not hinder, Cassius, your desires;
I'll leave you.

CASSIUS.

Brutus, I do observe you now of late:
I have not from your eyes that gentleness
And show of love as I was wont to have:[2]
You bear too stubborn and too strange[3] a hand
Over your friend that loves you.

MARCUS BRUTUS.

                       Cassius,
Be not deceived: if I have veil'd my look,
I turn the trouble of my countenance
Merely upon myself.[4] Vexed I am,
Of late, with passions of some difference,[5]
Conceptions only proper to myself,[6]
Which give some soil, perhaps, to my behaviours;

---

[1] the order of the course: how things transpire. [2] wont to have: used to have. [3] too stubborn and too strange: too hard and unusual. [4] if I have veil'd my look/ I turn the trouble of my countenance/ Merely upon myself: he has hidden his troublesome thoughts and kept them to himself. [5] passions of some difference: conflicting thoughts. [6] Conceptions only proper to myself: personal thoughts.

But let not therefore my good friends be grieved,—
Among which number, Cassius, be you one,—
Nor construe any further my neglect,
Than that poor Brutus, with himself at war,
Forgets the shows of love to other men.

CASSIUS.

Then, Brutus, I have much mistook your passion;[1]
By means whereof this breast of mine hath buried
Thoughts of great value, worthy cogitations.
Tell me, good Brutus, can you see your face?

MARCUS BRUTUS.

No, Cassius; for the eye sees not itself
But by reflection from some other thing.

CASSIUS.

'Tis just:[2]
And it is very much lamented, Brutus,
That you have no such mirrors as will turn
Your hidden worthiness into your eye,
That you might see your shadow. I have heard,
Where many of the best respect in Rome,—
Except immortal Cæsar,—speaking of Brutus,
And groaning underneath this age's yoke,
Have wisht that noble Brutus had his eyes.[3]

MARCUS BRUTUS.

Into what dangers would you lead me, Cassius,
That you would have me seek into myself
For that which is not in me?

CASSIUS.

Therefore, good Brutus, be prepared to hear:
And, since you know you cannot see yourself
So well as by reflection, I, your glass,[4]

---

[1] passion: state of mind; emotion.
[2] just: true.
[3] had his eyes: could see what was going on.
[4] glass: mirror.

Will modestly discover to yourself
That of yourself which you yet know not of.
And be not jealous on[1] me, gentle Brutus:
Were I a common laughter,[2] or did use
To stale[3] with ordinary oaths my love
To every new protester; if you know
That I do fawn on men, and hug them hard,
And after scandal [4] them; or if you know
That I profess myself in banqueting
To all the rout,[5] then hold me dangerous. [*Flourish and shout.*

    MARCUS BRUTUS.

What means this shouting? I do fear, the people
Choose Cæsar for their king.

    CASSIUS.

                    Ay, do you fear it?
Then must I think you would not have it so.

    MARCUS BRUTUS.

I would not, Cassius; yet I love him well.—
But wherefore do you hold me here so long?
What is it that you would impart to me?
If it be aught toward the general good,
Set honour in one eye, and death i'th'other,
And I will look on both indifferently;
For, let the gods so speed [6] me as I love
The name of honour more than I fear death.

    CASSIUS.

I know that virtue to be in you, Brutus,
As well as I do know your outward favour.[7]
Well, honour is the subject of my story.—
I cannot tell what you and other men
Think of this life; but, for my single self,

---

[1] **jealous on:** suspicious of. [2] **common laughter:** ordinary joker. [3] **to
stale:** to cheapen. [4] **scandal:** slander. [5] **rout:** disorderly company.
[6] **speed:** help; prosper. [7] **favour:** appearance.

I had as lief not be as live to be
In awe of such a thing as I myself.
I was born free as Cæsar; so were you:
We both have fed as well; and we can both
Endure the winter's cold as well as he:
For once, upon a raw and gusty day,
The troubled Tiber chafing with her shores,
Cæsar said to me, 'Darest thou, Cassius, now
Leap in with me into this angry flood,
And swim to yonder point?' Upon the word,
Accoutred [1] as I was, I plunged in,
And bade him follow: so, indeed, he did.
The torrent roar'd; and we did buffet it
With lusty sinews, throwing it aside
And stemming it with hearts of controversy: [2]
But ere we could arrive the point proposed,
Cæsar cried, 'Help me, Cassius, or I sink!'
I, as Aeneas, [3] our great ancestor,
Did from the flames of Troy upon his shoulder
The old Anchises [4] bear, so from the waves of Tiber
Did I the tired Cæsar: and this man
Is now become a god; and Cassius is
A wretched creature, and must bend his body,
If Cæsar carelessly but nod on him.
He had a fever when he was in Spain,
And, when the fit was on him, I did mark
How he did shake: 'tis true, this god did shake:
His coward lips did from their colour fly;
And that same eye, whose bend [5] doth awe the world,
Did lose his [6] lustre: I did hear him groan:
Ay, and that tongue of his, that bade the Romans

---

[1] Accoutred: equipped. [2] hearts of controversy: spirited contention. [3] Aeneas: mythical hero of Troy and Rome, son of the goddess Aphrodite and Anchises; Julius Caesar claimed descent from Aeneas. [4] Anchises: a member of the royal line at Troy. [5] bend: look. [6] his: its.

Mark him,[1] and write his speeches in their books,
Alas, it cried, 'Give me some drink, Titinius,'
As a sick girl. Ye gods, it doth amaze me,
A man of such a feeble temper should
So get the start of [2] the majestic world,
And bear the palm[3] alone.   [*Flourish and shout.*

     MARCUS BRUTUS.

Another general shout!
I do believe that these applauses are
For some new honours that are heapt on Cæsar.

      CASSIUS.

Why, man, he doth bestride the narrow world
Like a Colossus;[4] and we petty men
Walk under his huge legs, and peep about
To find ourselves dishonourable graves.
Men at some time are masters of their fates:
The fault, dear Brutus, is not in our stars,[5]
But in ourselves, that we are underlings.
Brutus, and Cæsar: what should be in that Cæsar?
Why should that name be sounded more than yours?
Write them together, yours is as fair a name;
Sound them, it doth become the mouth as well;
Weigh them, it is as heavy; conjure with 'em,
Brutus will start a spirit as soon as Cæsar.
Now, in the names of all the gods at once,
Upon what meat doth this our Cæsar feed,
That he is grown so great? Age,[6] thou art shamed!
Rome, thou hast lost the breed of noble bloods!
When went there by an age, since the great flood,
But it was famed with more than with one man?
When could they say, till now, that talkt of Rome,

---

[1] Mark him: pay attention to him. [2] get the start of: put himself ahead of. [3] palm: prize of victory. [4] Colossus: the giant statue of Apollo at Rhodes, so huge that ships could sail under its legs. [5] stars: fate; destiny. [6] Age: that particular period of time.

That her wide walls encompast but one man?
Now is it Rome indeed, and room enough,
When there is in it but one only man.
O, you and I have heard our fathers say,
There was a Brutus once that would have brookt[1]
Th'eternal devil to keep his state in Rome
As easily as a king.

    MARCUS BRUTUS.

That you do love me, I am nothing jealous;[2]
What you would work me to, I have some aim:[3]
How I have thought of this, and of these times,
I shall recount hereafter; for this present,
I would not, so with love I might entreat you,
Be any further moved. What you have said,
I will consider; what you have to say,
I will with patience hear; and find a time
Both meet[4] to hear and answer such high things.
Till then, my noble friend, chew upon this;
Brutus had rather be a villager
Than to repute himself a son of Rome
Under these hard conditions as this time
Is like to lay upon us.

    CASSIUS.

               I am glad
That my weak words have struck but thus much show
Of fire from Brutus.

    MARCUS BRUTUS.

The games are done, and Cæsar is returning.

    CASSIUS.

As they pass by, pluck Casca by the sleeve;
And he will, after his sour fashion, tell you
What hath proceeded worthy note to-day.

---

[1] brookt: endured; tolerated.
[2] I am nothing jealous: I have no doubt.
[3] aim: guess; conjecture.
[4] meet: suitable.

Enter CAESAR *and his* TRAIN.[1]

MARCUS BRUTUS.

I will do so:—but, look you, Cassius,
The angry spot doth glow on Cæsar's brow,
And all the rest look like a chidden[2] train:
Calphurnia's cheek is pale; and Cicero
Looks with such ferret[3] and such fiery eyes
As we have seen him in the Capitol,
Being crost in conference[4] by some senator.

CASSIUS.

Casca will tell us what the matter is.

JULIUS CAESAR.

Antonius,—

MARCUS ANTONIUS.

Cæsar?

JULIUS CAESAR.

Let me have men about me that are fat;
Sleek-headed men, and such as sleep o' nights:
Yond Cassius has a lean and hungry look;
He thinks too much: such men are dangerous.

MARCUS ANTONIUS.

Fear him not, Cæsar; he's not dangerous;
He is a noble Roman, and well given.[5]

JULIUS CAESAR.

Would he were fatter!—but I fear him not:
Yet if my name were liable to fear,
I do not know the man I should avoid
So soon as that spare Cassius. He reads much;
He is a great observer, and he looks
Quite through the deeds of men: he loves no plays,
As thou dost, Antony; he hears no music:

---

[1] train: retinue.
[2] chidden: scolded.
[3] ferret: red (as the eyes of a ferret).
[4] crost in conference: disputed.
[5] well given: well disposed; well mannered.

Seldom he smiles; and smiles in such a sort
As if he mockt himself, and scorn'd his spirit
That could be moved to smile at any thing.
Such men as he be never at heart's ease
Whiles they behold a greater than themselves;
And therefore are they very dangerous.
I rather tell thee what is to be fear'd
Than what I fear,—for always I am Cæsar.
Come on my right hand, for this ear is deaf,
And tell me truly what thou think'st of him.

                    [*Exeunt* CAESAR *and all his* TRAIN *but* CASCA.

 CASCA.

You pull'd me by the cloak; would you speak with me?

 MARCUS BRUTUS.

Ay, Casca; tell us what hath chanced [1] to-day,
That Cæsar looks so sad.

 CASCA.

Why, you were with him, were you not?

 MARCUS BRUTUS.

I should not, then, ask Casca what had chanced.

 CASCA.

Why, there was a crown offer'd him; and being offer'd him,
he put it by with the back of his hand, thus; and then the
people fell a-shouting.

 MARCUS BRUTUS.

What was the second noise for?

 CASCA.

Why, for that too.

 CASSIUS.

They shouted thrice: what was the last cry for?

---

[1] chanced: happened.

CASCA.

Why, for that too.

MARCUS BRUTUS.

Was the crown offer'd him thrice?

CASCA.

Ay, marry,[1] was't, and he put it by thrice, every time gentler than other; and at every putting-by mine honest neighbours shouted.

CASSIUS.

Who offer'd him the crown?

CASCA.

Why, Antony.

MARCUS BRUTUS.

Tell us the manner of it, gentle Casca.

CASCA.

I can as well be hang'd as tell the manner of it: it was mere foolery; I did not mark it. I saw Mark Antony offer him a crown;—yet 'twas not a crown neither, 'twas one of these coronets;—and, as I told you, he put it by[2] once: but, for all that, to my thinking, he would fain have had it.[3] Then he offer'd it to him again; then he put it by again: but, to my thinking, he was very loth to lay[4] his fingers off it. And then he offer'd it the third time; he put it the third time by; and still as he refused it, the rabblement shouted, and clapt their chopt hands, and threw up their sweaty nightcaps, and utter'd such a deal of stinking breath because Cæsar refused the crown, that it had almost choked Cæsar; for he swounded,[5] and fell down at it: and for my own part, I durst not laugh, for fear of opening my lips and receiving the bad air.

---

[1] marry: mild oath—by the Virgin Mary!
[2] put it by: pushed it away.
[3] he would fain have had it: he would have liked to have it.
[4] lay: keep.
[5] swounded: fainted; swooned.

CASSIUS.

But, soft, I pray you: what, did Cæsar swound?

CASCA.

He fell down in the market-place, and foam'd at mouth, and was speechless.

MARCUS BRUTUS.

'Tis very like;—he hath the falling-sickness.[1]

CASSIUS.

No, Cæsar hath it not: but you, and I,
And honest Casca, we have the falling-sickness.

CASCA.

I know not what you mean by that; but, I am sure, Cæsar fell down. If the tag-rag people[2] did not clap him and hiss him, according as he pleased and displeased them, as they use to do the players in the theatre, I am no true man.

MARCUS BRUTUS.

What said he when he came unto himself?

CASCA.

Marry, before he fell down, when he perceived the common herd was glad he refused the crown, he pluckt me ope[3] his doublet, and offer'd them his throat to cut:—an[4] I had been a man of any occupation, if I would not have taken him at a word, I would I might go to hell among the rogues:—and so he fell. When he came to himself again, he said, if he had done or said any thing amiss, he desired their worships to think it was his infirmity. Three or four wenches, where I stood, cried, 'Alas, good soul!' and forgave him with all their hearts: but there's no heed to be taken of them; if Cæsar had stabb'd their mothers, they would have done no less.

---

[1] falling-sickness: epileptic seizure.
[2] tag-rag people: the common people.
[3] pluckt me ope: plucked open.
[4] an: if.

MARCUS BRUTUS.

And after that, he came, thus sad, away?

CASCA.

Ay.

CASSIUS.

Did Cicero say any thing?

CASCA.

Ay, he spoke Greek.

CASSIUS.

To what effect?

CASCA.

Nay, an I tell you that, I'll ne'er look you i'th' face again: but those that understood him smiled at one another, and shook their heads; but, for mine own part, it was Greek to me.[1] I could tell you more news too: Marullus and Flavius, for pulling scarfs off Cæsar's images, are put to silence. Fare you well. There was more foolery yet, if I could remember it.

CASSIUS.

Will you sup with me to-night, Casca?

CASCA.

No, I am promised forth.

CASSIUS.

Will you dine with me to-morrow?

CASCA.

Ay, if I be alive, and your mind hold, and your dinner worth the eating.

CASSIUS.

Good; I will expect you.

---

[1] Greek to me: unintelligible to me.

CASCA.

Do so: farewell, both.   [*Exit.*

MARCUS BRUTUS.

What a blunt fellow is this grown to be!
He was quick mettle[1] when he went to school.

CASSIUS.

So is he now, in execution
Of any bold or noble enterprise,
However he puts on this tardy form.[2]
This rudeness is a source to his good wit,
Which gives men stomach to digest his words
With better appetite.

MARCUS BRUTUS.

And so it is. For this time I will leave you:
To-morrow, if you please to speak with me,
I will come home to you; or, if you will,
Come home to me, and I will wait for you.

CASSIUS.

I will do so:—till then, think of the world.   [*Exit* BRUTUS.
Well Brutus, thou art noble; yet, I see,
Thy honourable mettle may be wrought
From that it is disposed:[3] therefore 'tis meet
That noble minds keep ever with their likes;[4]
For who so firm that cannot be seduced?
Cæsar doth bear me hard;[5] but he loves Brutus:
If I were Brutus now, and he were Cassius,
He should not humour me. I will this night,
In several hands,[6] in at his windows throw,
As if they came from several citizens,
Writings, all tending to the great opinion
That Rome holds of his name; wherein obscurely
Cæsar's ambition shall be glanced at:[7]

---

[1] quick mettle: quick-witted. [2] However he puts on this tardy form:
even though he assumes this sluggish manner. [3] From that it is
disposed: changed from its natural bent. [4] likes: equals. [5] doth
bear me hard: bears ill-will against me. [6] several hands: in several
different handwritings. [7] glanced at: hinted at.

And, after this, let Cæsar seat him sure;[1]
For we will shake him, or worse days endure.   [*Exit.*

SCENE III.

The same. A street.

Thunder and lightning. Enter, from opposite sides, CASCA, with his sword drawn, and CICERO.

CICERO.

Good even, Casca: brought you Cæsar home?
Why are you breathless? and why stare you so?

CASCA.

Are not you moved, when all the sway of earth
Shakes like a thing unfirm? O Cicero,
I have seen tempests, when the scolding winds
Have rived [2] the knotty oaks; and I have seen
Th'ambitious ocean swell and rage and foam,
To be exalted with the threat'ning clouds:
But never till to-night, never till now,
Did I go through a tempest dropping fire.
Either there is a civil strife in heaven;
Or else the world, too saucy with the gods,
Incenses them to send destruction.

CICERO.

Why, saw you any thing more wonderful?

CASCA.

A common slave—you know him well by sight—
Held up his left hand, which did flame and burn
Like twenty torches join'd; and yet his hand,
Not sensible[3] of fire, remain'd unscorcht.
Besides,—I ha' not since put up my sword,—
Against the Capitol I met a lion,

---

[1] seat him sure: make his position secure.
[2] rived: split.
[3] sensible: aware.

Who glared upon me, and went surly by,
Without annoying me: and there were drawn
Upon a heap[1] a hundred ghastly women,
Transformed with their fear; who swore they saw
Men, all in fire, walk up and down the streets.
And yesterday the bird of night[2] did sit
Even at noonday upon the market-place,
Hooting and shrieking. When these prodigies[3]
Do so conjointly[4] meet, let not men say,
'These are their reasons,—they are natural;'
For, I believe, they are portentous things
Unto the climate[5] that they point upon.

CICERO.

Indeed, it is a strange-disposed time:
But men may construe things after their fashion,
Clean from the purpose of the things themselves.[6]
Comes Cæsar to the Capitol to-morrow?

CASCA.

He doth; for he did bid Antonius
Send word to you he would be there to-morrow.

CICERO.

Good night, then, Casca: this disturbed sky
Is not to walk in.

CASCA.

                    Farewell, Cicero.   [*Exit* CICERO.

                    Enter CASSIUS.

CASSIUS.
Who's there?

CASCA.
          A Roman.

CASSIUS.
                    Casca, by your voice.

---

[1] **drawn/ Upon a heap:** gathered closely together. [2] **bird of night:** the owl. [3] **prodigies:** unnatural things. [4] **conjointly:** simultaneously. [5] **climate:** region. [6] **construe things after their fashion,/ Clean from the purpose of the things themselves:** men sometimes believe what they want to believe, instead of the truth.

CASCA.

Your ear is good. Cassius, what night is this!

CASSIUS.

A very pleasing night to honest men.

CASCA.

Who ever knew the heavens menace so?

CASSIUS.

Those that have known the earth so full of faults.
For my part, I have walkt about the streets,
Submitting me unto the perilous night;
And, thus unbraced,[1] Casca, as you see,
Have bared by bosom to the thunder-stone:[2]
And when the cross blue lightning seem'd to open
The breast of heaven, I did present[3] myself
Even in the aim and very flash of it.

CASCA.

But wherefore did you so much tempt the heavens?
It is the part of men to fear and tremble,
When the most mighty gods by tokens send
Such dreadful heralds to astonish us.[4]

CASSIUS.

You are dull, Casca; and those sparks of life
That should be in a Roman you do want,[5]
Or else you use not. You look pale, and gaze,
And put on fear, and cast yourself in wonder,
To see the strange impatience[6] of the heavens:
But if you would consider the true cause
Why all these fires, why all these gliding ghosts,
Why birds and beasts from quality and kind [7]—
Why old men, fools, and children calculate;[8]
Why all these things change from their ordinance,[9]

---

[1] **unbraced:** unbuttoned, or unfastened. [2] **thunder-stone:** thunder-bolt. [3] **present:** expose. [4] **astonish us:** stun us with terror. [5] **want:** lack. [6] **impatience:** restlessness; turbulence. [7] **from quality and kind:** not according to their usual disposition. [8] **calculate:** speculate upon future events. [9] **ordinance:** normal or ordinary pattern of behavior.

Their natures, and pre-formed faculties,
To monstrous[1] quality;—why, you shall find
That heaven hath infused them with these spirits,
To make them instruments of fear and warning
Unto some monstrous state.
Now could I, Casca, name to thee a man
Most like this dreadful night,
That thunders, lightens, opens graves, and roars
As doth the lion in the Capitol,—
A man no mightier than thyself or me
In personal action; yet prodigious grown,
And fearful, as these strange eruptions[2] are.

    CASCA.

'Tis Cæsar that you mean; is it not, Cassius?

    CASSIUS.

Let it be who it is; for Romans now
Have thews[3] and limbs like to their ancestors;
But, woe the while![4] our fathers' minds are dead,
And we are govern'd with our mothers' spirits;[5]
Our yoke and sufferance[6] show us womanish.

    CASCA.

Indeed, they say the senators to-morrow
Mean to establish Cæsar as a king;
And he shall wear his crown by sea and land,
In every place, save here in Italy.

    CASSIUS.

I know where I will wear this dagger, then;
Cassius from bondage will deliver Cassius:
Therein, ye gods, you make the weak most strong;
Therein, ye gods, you tyrants do defeat:
Nor stony tower, nor walls of beaten brass

---

[1] monstrous: unnatural.
[2] eruptions: events.
[3] thews: muscles; sinews.
[4] woe the while: alas the time.
[5] mothers' spirits: timidity.
[6] yoke: symbol of bondage; **sufferance**: endurance of bondage.

Nor airless dungeon, nor strong links of iron,
Can be retentive to the strength of spirit;
But life, being weary of these worldly bars,
Never lacks power to dismiss[1] itself.
If I know this, know all the world besides,
That part of tyranny that I do bear
I can shake off at pleasure.[2]   [*Thunder still.*

    CASCA.

              So can I:
So every bondman[3] in his own hand bears
The power to cancel his captivity.

    CASSIUS.

And why should Cæsar be a tyrant, then?
Poor man! I know he would not be a wolf,
But that he sees the Romans are but sheep:
He were no lion, were not Romans hinds.[4]
Those that with haste will make a mighty fire
Begin it with weak straws: what trash is Rome,
What rubbish, and what offal, when it serves
For the base matter to illuminate[5]
So vile a thing as Cæsar! But, O grief,
Where hast thou led me? I perhaps speak this
Before a willing bondman: then I know
My answer must be made; but I am arm'd,[6]
And dangers are to me indifferent.

    CASCA.

You speak to Casca; and to such a man
That is no fleering[7] tell-tale. Hold, my hand:
Be factious[8] for redress of all these griefs;
And I will set this foot of mine as far
As who goes farthest.

---

[1] **dismiss**: free. [2] **at pleasure**: at my choosing. [3] **bondman**: slave.
[4] **hinds**: female red deer; hence, timid, or cowardly. [5] **illuminate**:
add to his luster. [6] **arm'd**: prepared. [7] **fleering**: grinning; scornful.
[8] **factious**: partisan.

CASSIUS.

There's a bargain made.
Now know you, Casca, I have moved already
Some certain of the noblest-minded Romans
To undergo with me an enterprise
Of honourable-dangerous consequence;
And I do know, by this, they stay[1] for me
In Pompey's porch:[2] for now, this fearful night,
There is no stir or walking in the streets;
And the complexion[3] of the element
In's favour's[4] like the work we have in hand,
Most bloody, fiery and most terrible.

CASCA.

Stand close[5] awhile, for here comes one in haste.

CASSIUS.

'Tis Cinna,—I do know him by his gait;
He is a friend.

Enter CINNA.

Cinna, where haste you so?

CINNA.

To find out you. Who's that? Metellus Cimber?

CASSIUS.

No, it is Casca; one incorporate
To our attempts.[6] Am I not stay'd for,[7] Cinna?

CINNA.

I am glad on't.[8] What a fearful night is this!
There's two or three of us have seen strange sights.

CASSIUS.

Am I not stay'd for? tell me.

CINNA.

Yes, you are.—

---

[1] stay: wait. [2] Pompey's porch: the portico of Pompey's Theatre, in
the Campus Martius; *Porticus Pompeii.* [3] complexion: nature.
[4] favour: appearance. [5] close: hidden. [6] one incorporate/ To our
attempts: one who is joined in our enterprise. [7] stay'd for: awaited.
[8] on't: of it.

O Cassius, if you could
But win the noble Brutus to our party—

CASSIUS.

Be you content:[1] good Cinna, take this paper,
And look you lay it in the prætor's chair,
Where Brutus may but find it; and throw this
In at his window; set this up with wax
Upon old Brutus' statue: all this done,
Repair to[2] Pompey's porch, where you shall find us.
Is Decius Brutus and Trebonius there?

CINNA.

All but Metellus Cimber; and he's gone
To seek you at your house. Well, I will hie,[3]
And so bestow these papers as you bade me.

CASSIUS.

That done, repair to Pompey's theatre.   [Exit CINNA.
Come, Casca, you and I will yet, ere day,
See Brutus at his house: three parts of him
Is ours already; and the man entire,
Upon the next encounter, yields him ours.[4]

CASCA.

O, he sits high in all the people's hearts:
And that which would appear offence in us,
His countenance,[5] like richest alchemy,[6]
Will change to virtue and to worthiness.

CASSIUS.

Him, and his worth, and our great need of him,
You have right well conceited.[7] Let us go,
For it is after midnight; and, ere day,
We will awake him, and be sure of him.   [Exeunt.

---

[1] content: easy. [2] repair to: go to. [3] hie: hurry. [4] yields him ours: becomes our man. [5] countenance: approval. [6] richest alchemy: the magic of changing base metals to gold. [7] conceited: conceived.

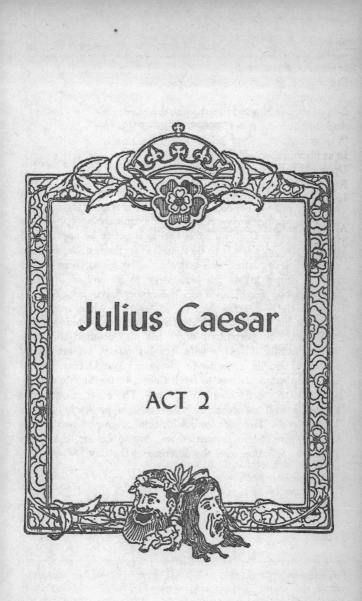

Julius Caesar

ACT 2

ACT II

ALONE in the garden of his house, Brutus persuades himself
to act for what seems to him public necessity even though
this will involve personal betrayal and the murder of a man
who has not yet condemned himself as a tyrant. Cassius and
the conspirators arrive furtively, and quickly accept Brutus
as their leader. On his advice, Cicero is not to be approached
to join, Antony's life is to be spared even though Cassius, the
more efficient plotter, sees a probable danger to them in this
mercy. Brutus insists the plot is not to be one of butchery
but a public sacrifice. When the others have left, Brutus's
wife Portia reproaches him for his secrecy when something
preys on his mind, until Brutus is willing to share his trouble
with her. The portentous night has also aroused the fears
of Calphurnia, Caesar's wife, for his safety. Caesar finally
agrees to remain at home to please her but Decius, one of
the conspirators, arrives to fetch Caesar to the Senate and by
adroit flattery persuades him to come. The other conspirators
arrive as well to accompany Caesar in a procession to the
senate house. The act closes with brief scenes of two people
waiting, one to give a written warning to Caesar, the other,
Portia, in agitation over the outcome of the day.

ACT II. Scene I.

Rome. BRUTUS' *orchard.*

Enter MARCUS BRUTUS.

MARCUS BRUTUS.
What, Lucius, ho!—
I cannot, by the progress of the stars,
Give guess how near to day.—Lucius, I say!—
I would it were my fault to sleep so soundly.—
When, Lucius, when? awake, I say! what, Lucius!

Enter LUCIUS.

LUCIUS.
Call'd you, my lord?
MARCUS BRUTUS.
Get me a taper[1] in my study, Lucius:
When it is lighted, come and call me here.
LUCIUS.
I will, my lord.   [*Exit.*
MARCUS BRUTUS.
It must be by his death: and, for my part,
I know no personal cause to spurn at[2] him,
But for the general. He would be crown'd:[3]—
How that might change his nature, there's the question:
It is the bright day that brings forth the adder;[4]
And that craves wary walking. Crown him?—that;—

---

[1] taper: candle.
[2] spurn at: to turn against.
[3] He would be crown'd: he would like to wear the crown.
[4] adder: snake.

And then, I grant, we put a sting in him,
That at his will he may do danger with.
Th'abuse of greatness is, when it disjoins
Remorse from power: and, to speak truth of Cæsar,
I have not known when his affections sway'd [1]
More than his reason. But 'tis a common proof, [2]
That lowliness is young ambition's ladder,
Whereto the climber-upward turns his face;
But when he once attains the upmost round,
He then unto the ladder turns his back,
Looks in the clouds, scorning the base degrees
By which he did ascend: so Cæsar may;
Then, lest he may, prevent. And, since the quarrel
Will bear no colour for the thing he is, [3]
Fashion it thus; that what he is, augmented,
Would run to these and these extremities:
And therefore think him as a serpent's egg,
Which, hatcht, would, as his kind, grow mischievous; [4]
And kill him in the shell.

Enter LUCIUS.

LUCIUS.
The taper burneth in your closet, [5] sir.
Searching the window for a flint, I found
                             [*Gives him the letter.*
This paper, thus seal'd up; and, I am sure,
It did not lie there when I went to bed.
    MARCUS BRUTUS.
Get you to bed again; it is not day.
Is not to-morrow, boy, the ides of March?

---

[1] sway'd: were influenced. [2] common proof: well-known and tested fact. [3] And, since the quarrel/ Will bear no colour for the thing he is: the public image of Caesar is such that an action so contemptible would not be condoned. [4] mischievous: harmful. [5] closet: chamber; room.

LUCIUS.

I know not, sir.

MARCUS BRUTUS.

Look in the calendar, and bring me word.

LUCIUS.

I will, sir.   [*Exit.*

MARCUS BRUTUS.

The exhalations,[1] whizzing in the air,
Give so much light, that I may read by them.

[*Opens the letter and reads.*

'Brutus, thou sleep'st; awake, and see thyself.
Shall Rome, &c. Speak, strike, redress!'—
'Brutus, thou sleep'st: awake!'—
Such instigations have been often dropt
Where I have took them up.
'Shall Rome, &c.' Thus must I piece it out;[2]
Shall Rome stand under one man's awe? What, Rome?
My ancestors did from the streets of Rome
The Tarquin[3] drive, when he was call'd a king.
'Speak, strike, redress!'—Am I entreated
To speak and strike? O Rome, I make thee promise,
If the redress will follow, thou receivest
Thy full petition at the hand of Brutus!

Enter LUCIUS.

LUCIUS.

Sir, March is wasted fifteen days.   [*Knock within.*

MARCUS BRUTUS.

'Tis good. Go to the gate; somebody knocks,   [*Exit* LUCIUS.
Since Cassius first did whet me against Cæsar,

---

[1] exhalations: meteors; shooting stars.
[2] piece it out: fill it in.
[3] Tarquin: Lucius Tarquinius Superbus, the seventh and last legendary king of ancient Rome.

I have not slept.
Between the acting of a dreadful thing
And the first motion,[1] all the interim is
Like a phantasma or a hideous dream:
The Genius[2] and the mortal instruments[3]
Are then in council; and the state of man,
Like to a little kingdom, suffers then
The nature of an insurrection.

Enter LUCIUS.

LUCIUS.
Sir, 'tis your brother Cassius at the door,
Who doth desire to see you.

MARCUS BRUTUS.
                Is he alone?

LUCIUS.
No, sir, there are moe[4] with him.

MARCUS BRUTUS.
             Do you know them?

LUCIUS.
No, sir; their hats are pluckt[5] about their ears,
And half their faces buried in their cloaks,
That by no means I may discover them
By any mark of favour.[6]

MARCUS BRUTUS.
            Let 'em enter.   [*Exit* LUCIUS.
They are the faction. O conspiracy,
Shamest thou to show thy dangerous brow by night,
When evils are most free? O, then, by day
Where wilt thou find a cavern dark enough
To mask thy monstrous visage? Seek none, conspiracy;

---

[1] motion: move. [2] The Genius: the rational spirit temporarily lodged in the body, directing it for good or evil. [3] mortal instruments: deadly impulses. [4] moe: more. [5] pluckt: pulled down. [6] favour: countenance.

Hide it in smiles and affability:
For if thou put thy native semblance on,[1]
Not Erebus[2] itself were dim enough
To hide thee from prevention.

Enter the Conspirators, CASSIUS, CASCA, DECIUS, CINNA,
METELLUS CIMBER, *and* TREBONIUS.

CASSIUS.

I think we are too bold upon your rest:
Good morrow, Brutus; do we trouble you?

MARCUS BRUTUS.

I have been up this hour; awake all night.
Know I these men that come along with you?

CASSIUS.

Yes, every man of them; and no man here
But honours you; and every one doth wish
You had but that opinion of yourself
Which every noble Roman bears of you—
This is Trebonius.

MARCUS BRUTUS.

He is welcome hither.

CASSIUS.

This, Decius Brutus.

MARCUS BRUTUS.

He is welcome too.

CASSIUS.

This, Casca; this, Cinna; and this, Metellus Cimber.

MARCUS BRUTUS.

They are all welcome.—
What watchful cares do interpose themselves
Betwixt your eyes and night? [3]

---

[1] **put thy native semblance on:** go in without disguise; in a normal
way.
[2] **Erebus:** in Greek Mythology, the region of utter darkness through
which the soul passes on its way from Earth to Hades.
[3] **What watchful cares do interpose themselves/ Betwixt your eyes
and night?:** what grave problems keep you from sleeping?

CASSIUS.

Shall I entreat a word?   [*They whisper.*

DECIUS BRUTUS.

Here lies the east: doth not the day break here?

CASCA.

No.

CINNA.

O, pardon, sir, it doth; and yon gray lines
That fret[1] the clouds are messengers of day.

CASCA.

You shall confess that you are both deceived.
Here, as I point my sword, the sun arises;
Which is a great way growing on[2] the south,
Weighing[3] the youthful season of the year.
Some two months hence, up higher toward the north
He first presents his fire; and the high east
Stands, as the Capitol, directly here.

MARCUS BRUTUS.

Give me your hands all over, one by one.

CASSIUS.

And let us swear our resolution.

MARCUS BRUTUS.

No, not an oath: if not the face of men,[4]
The sufferance of our souls, the time's abuse,[5]—
If these be motives weak, break off betimes,[6]
And every man hence to his idle bed;
So let high-sighted[7] tyranny range on,
Till each man drop by lottery.[8] But if these,
As I am sure they do, bear fire enough
To kindle cowards, and to steel with valour
The melting spirits of women; then, countrymen,

---

[1] fret: variegate (as in fretwork). [2] growing on: encroaching on.
[3] Weighing: taking into consideration. [4] face of men: public opinion.
[5] time's abuse: the abuses of the time. [6] betimes: in good time.
[7] high-sighted: haughty; supercilious. [8] each man drop by lottery:
each man die in turn.

What need we any spur, but our own cause,
To prick[1] us to redress? what other bond
Than secret Romans, that have spoke the word,
And will not palter?[2] and what other oath
Than honesty to honesty engaged,[3]
That this shall be, or we will fall for it?
Swear priests, and cowards, and men cautelous,[4]
Old feeble carrions, and such suffering souls
That welcome wrongs; unto bad causes swear
Such creatures as men doubt: but do not stain
The even[5] virtue of our enterprise,
Nor th'insuppressive[6] mettle of our spirits,
To think that or our cause or our performance
Did need an oath; when every drop of blood
That every Roman bears, and nobly bears,
Is guilty of a several bastardy,
If he do break the smallest particle
Of any promise that hath past from him.

CASSIUS.

But what of Cicero? shall we sound him?
I think he will stand very strong with us.

CASCA.

Let us not leave him out.

CINNA.

No, by no means.

METELLUS CIMBER.

O, let us have him; for his silver hairs
Will purchase us a good opinion,
And buy men's voices to commend our deeds:
It shall be said, his judgement ruled our hands;
Our youths and wildness shall no whit appear,
But all be buried in his gravity.

---

[1] **prick**: incite. [2] **palter**: equivocate. [3] **honesty to honesty engaged**: honest men embarked on an honorable cause. [4] **cautelous**: crafty; cautious. [5] **even**: pure; unblemished. [6] **insuppressive**: not to be suppressed.

MARCUS BRUTUS.

O, name him not: let us not break with him;[1]
For he will never follow any thing
That other men begin.

CASSIUS.

                Then leave him out.

CASCA.

Indeed he is not fit.[2]

DECIUS BRUTUS.

Shall no man else be toucht but only Cæsar?

CASSIUS.

Decius, well urged:[3]—I think it is not meet,[4]
Mark Antony, so well beloved of Cæsar,
Should outlive Cæsar: we shall find of[5] him
A shrewd contriver; and, you know, his means,[6]
If he improve them, may well stretch so far
As to annoy us all: which to prevent,
Let Antony and Cæsar fall together.

MARCUS BRUTUS.

Our course will seem too bloody, Caius Cassius,
To cut the head off, and then hack the limbs,—
Like wrath in death, and envy[7] afterwards;
For Antony is but a limb of Cæsar:
Let's be sacrificers, but not butchers, Caius.
We all stand up against the spirit of Cæsar;
And in the spirit of men there is no blood:
O, that we, then, could come by[8] Cæsar's spirit,
And not dismember Cæsar! But, alas,
Cæsar must bleed for it! And, gentle friends,
Let's kill him boldly, but not wrathfully;
Let's carve him as a dish fit for the gods,

---

[1] **break with him:** broach the subject to him. [2] **fit:** worthy. [3] **urged:** presented. [4] **meet:** proper. [5] **of:** in. [6] **means:** capabilities. [7] **envy:** hatred; malice. [8] **come by:** get possession of; influence.

Not hew him as a carcass fit for hounds:
And let our hearts, as subtle masters do,
Stir up their servants to an act of rage,
And after seem to chide 'em. This shall make
Our purpose necessary, and not envious:
Which so appearing to the common eyes,
We shall be call'd purgers, not murderers.
And for Mark Antony, think not of him;
For he can do no more than Cæsar's arm
When Cæsar's head is off.

      CASSIUS.

                  Yet I fear him;
For in the ingrafted [1] love he bears to Cæsar—

      MARCUS BRUTUS.

Alas, good Cassius, do not think of him:
If he love Cæsar, all that he can do
Is to himself,—take thought,[2] and die for Cæsar:
And that were much[3] he should; for he is given
To sports, to wildness, and much company.

      TREBONIUS.

There is no fear in him;[4] let him not die;
For he will live, and laugh at this hereafter.   [Clock strikes.

      MARCUS BRUTUS.

Peace! count the clock.

      CASSIUS.

               The clock hath stricken three.

      TREBONIUS.

'Tis time to part.

      CASSIUS.

             But it is doubtful yet,
Whether Cæsar will come forth to-day or no;

---

[1] **ingrafted:** ingrained; strong.
[2] **take thought:** mourn; grieve; give way to melancholy.
[3] **were much:** not likely; too much to expect.
[4] **There is no fear in him:** he is not to be feared.

For he is superstitious grown of late;
Quite from the main[1] opinion he held once
Of fantasy, of dreams, and ceremonies:[2]
It may be, these apparent prodigies,[3]
The unaccustom'd terror of this night,
And the persuasion of his augurers,[4]
May hold him from the Capitol to-day.

DECIUS BRUTUS.

Never fear that: if he be so resolved,
I can o'ersway him; for he loves to hear
That unicorns[5] may be betray'd with trees,
And bears with glasses,[6] elephants with holes,[7]
Lions with toils,[8] and men with flatterers:
But when I tell him he hates flatterers,
He says he does,—being then most flattered.
Let me work;
For I can give his humour[9] the true bent,[10]
And I will bring him to the Capitol.

CASSIUS.

Nay, we will all of us be there to fetch him.

MARCUS BRUTUS.

By the eighth hour: is that the uttermost?

CINNA.

Be that the uttermost, and fail not then.

METELLUS CIMBER.

Caius Ligarius doth bear Cæsar hard,[11]
Who rated [12] him for speaking well of Pompey:
I wonder none of you have thought of him.

MARCUS BRUTUS.

Now, good Metellus, go along by[13] him:
He loves me well, and I have given him reasons;
Send him but hither, and I'll fashion him.

---

[1] main: confident; firm. [2] ceremonies: omens. [3] apparent prodigies: manifest omens. [4] augurers: professional interpreters of omens. [5] unicorn: a mythical, horselike animal with a single horn in the middle of its forehead. [6] glasses: mirrors. [7] holes: concealed pits. [8] toils: nets; snares. [9] humour: caprice. [10] bent: inclination. [11] bear Caesar hard: bears ill-will against Caesar. [12] rated: berated. [13] by: to.

CASSIUS.

The morning comes upon's: we'll leave you, Brutus:—
And, friends, disperse yourselves; but all remember
What you have said, and show yourselves true Romans.

MARCUS BRUTUS.

Good gentlemen, look fresh and merrily;
Let not our looks put on[1] our purposes;
But bear it as our Roman actors do,
With untired spirits and formal constancy:[2]
And so, good morrow to you every one.

[*Exeunt all but* BRUTUS.

Boy! Lucius!—Fast asleep? It is no matter;
Enjoy the honey-heavy dew of slumber:
Thou hast no figures nor no fantasies,
Which busy care draws in the brains of men;
Therefore thou sleep'st so sound.

Enter PORTIA.

PORTIA.

Brutus, my lord!

MARCUS BRUTUS.

Portia, what mean you? wherefore rise you now?
It is not for your health[3] thus to commit
Your weak condition to the raw-cold morning.

PORTIA.

Nor for yours neither. Y' have ungently,[4] Brutus,
Stole from my bed: and yesternight, at supper,
You suddenly arose, and walkt about,
Musing and sighing, with your arms across;
And when I askt you what the matter was,
You stared upon me with ungentle looks:

---

[1] put on: betray.
[2] formal constancy: proper or normal composure.
[3] not for your health: not healthy.
[4] ungently: unkindly; impolitely.

I urged you further; then you scratcht your head,
And too impatiently stampt with your foot:
Yet I insisted, yet you answer'd not;
But, with an angry wafture[1] of your hand,
Gave sign for me to leave you: so I did;
Fearing to strengthen that impatience
Which seem'd too much enkindled; and withal
Hoping it was but an effect of humour,[2]
Which sometime hath his hour with every man.
It will not let you eat, nor talk, nor sleep;
And, could it work so much upon your shape,
As it hath much prevail'd on your condition,
I should not know you, Brutus. Dear my lord,
Make me acquainted with your cause of grief.

    MARCUS BRUTUS.

I am not well in health, and that is all.

    PORTIA.

Brutus is wise, and, were he not in health,
He would embrace the means to come by it.

    MARCUS BRUTUS.

Why, so I do.—Good Portia, go to bed.

    PORTIA.

Is Brutus sick,—and is it physical[3]
To walk unbraced,[4] and suck up the humours
Of the dank morning? What, is Brutus sick,—
And will he steal out of his wholesome bed,
To dare the vile contagion of the night,
And tempt the rheumy and unpurged[5] air
To add unto his sickness? No, my Brutus;
You have some sick offence within your mind,[6]
Which, by the right and virtue of my place,

---

[1] **wafture:** waving.
[2] **humour:** caprice.
[3] **physical:** healthy.
[4] **unbraced:** unbuttoned.
[5] **unpurged:** not purified by the sun; unwholesome.
[6] **sick offence within your mind:** troublesome, sickening worry.

I ought to know of: and, upon my knees,
I charm[1] you, by my once-commended beauty,
By all your vows of love, and that great vow
Which did incorporate and make us one,
That you unfold to me, yourself, your half,
Why you are heavy;[2] and what men to-night
Have had resort to you,—for here have been
Some six or seven, who did hide their faces
Even from darkness.

    MARCUS BRUTUS.

               Kneel not, gentle Portia.

    PORTIA.

I should not need, if you were gentle Brutus.
Within the bond of marriage, tell me, Brutus,
Is it excepted I should know no secrets
That appertain to you? Am I yourself
But, as it were, in sort or limitation,—
To keep with you at meals, comfort your bed,
And talk to you sometimes? Dwell I but in the suburbs
Of your good pleasure? If it be no more,
Portia is Brutus' harlot, not his wife.

    MARCUS BRUTUS.

You are my true and honourable wife;
As dear to me as are the ruddy drops[3]
That visit my sad heart.

    PORTIA.

If this were true, then should I know this secret.
I grant I am a woman; but withal
A woman that Lord Brutus took to wife:
I grant I am a woman; but withal
A woman well-reputed,—Cato's daughter.
Think you I am no stronger than my sex,

---

[1] charm: conjure; implore.
[2] heavy: troubled; depressed.
[3] ruddy drops: red drops (blood).

Being so father'd and so husbanded?
Tell me your counsels;[1] I will not disclose 'em:
I have made strong proof of my constancy,[2]
Giving myself a voluntary wound
Here, in the thigh: can I bear that with patience,
And not my husband's secrets?

MARCUS BRUTUS.

                 O ye gods,
Render me worthy of this noble wife!   [Knock.
Hark, hark! one knocks: Portia, go in awhile;
And by and by thy bosom shall partake
The secrets of my heart:
All my engagements[3] I will construe to thee,
All the charactery[4] of my sad brows:—
Leave me with haste. [Exit PORTIA.]—Lucius, who's that
knocks?

Enter LUCIUS *with* LIGARIUS.

LUCIUS.

Here is a sick man that would speak with you.

MARCUS BRUTUS.

Caius Ligarius, that Metellus spake of.—
Boy, stand aside.—Caius Ligarius,—how!

LIGARIUS.

Vouchsafe[5] good-morrow from a feeble tongue.

MARCUS BRUTUS.

O, what a time have you chose out, brave Caius,
To wear a kerchief! Would you were not sick!

LIGARIUS.

I am not sick, if Brutus have in hand
Any exploit worthy the name of honour.

MARCUS BRUTUS.

Such an exploit have I in hand, Ligarius,

---

[1] counsels: secrets.
[2] constancy: fortitude.
[3] engagements: projects.
[4] charactery: signs used in the expression of thought; meaning.
[5] Vouchsafe: deign to accept.

Had you a healthful ear to hear of it.

    LIGARIUS.

By all the gods that Romans bow before,
I here discard my sickness! Soul of Rome!
Brave son, derived from honourable loins!
Thou, like an exorcist, hast conjured up
My mortified [1] spirit. Now bid me run,
And I will strive[2] with things impossible;
Yea, get the better of them. What's to do?

    MARCUS BRUTUS.

A piece of work that will make sick men whole.

    LIGARIUS.

But are not some whole that we must make sick?

    MARCUS BRUTUS.

That must we also. What it is, my Caius,
I shall unfold to thee, as we are going
To whom it must be done.   .

    LIGARIUS.

                Set on your foot;
And, with a heart new-fired, I follow you,
To do I know not what: but it sufficeth
That Brutus leads me on.

    MARCUS BRUTUS.

                Follow me, then.   [*Exeunt.*

Scene II.

The same. A hall in CAESAR'S *palace.*

Thunder and lightning. Enter JULIUS CAESAR, *in his nightgown.*

    JULIUS CAESAR.

Nor heaven nor earth have been at peace to-night:

---

[1] mortified: deadened.
[2] strive: contend.

Thrice hath Calphurnia in her sleep cried out,
'Help, ho! they murder Cæsar!'—Who's within?

Enter a SERVANT.

SERVANT.
My lord?
    JULIUS CAESAR.
Go bid the priests do present[1] sacrifice,
And bring me their opinions of success.
    SERVANT.
I will, my lord.   [*Exit.*

Enter CALPHURNIA.

CALPHURNIA.
What mean you, Cæsar? think you to walk forth?
You shall not stir out of your house to-day.
    JULIUS CAESAR.
Cæsar shall forth: the things that threaten'd me
Ne'er lookt but on my back; when they shall see
The face of Cæsar, they are vanished.
    CALPHURNIA.
Cæsar, I never stood on ceremonies,[2]
Yet now they fright me. There is one within,
Besides the things that we have heard and seen,
Recounts most horrid sights seen by the watch.
A lioness hath whelped [3] in the streets;
And graves have yawn'd, and yielded up their dead;
Fierce fiery warriors fight upon the clouds,
In ranks and squadrons and right form of war,[4]
Which drizzled blood upon the Capitol;
The noise of battle hurtled in the air,
Horses did neigh, and dying men did groan;

---

[1] present: immediate.
[2] stood on ceremonies: believed in omens.
[3] whelped: given birth.
[4] right form of war: proper battle procedure; battle formation.

And ghosts did shriek and squeal about the streets.
O Cæsar, these things are beyond all use,[1]
And I do fear them!

    JULIUS CAESAR.

                What can be avoided
Whose end is purposed by the mighty gods?
Yet Cæsar shall go forth; for these predictions
Are to the world in general as to Cæsar.

    CALPHURNIA.

When beggars die, there are no comets seen;
The heavens themselves blaze forth the death of princes.

    JULIUS CAESAR.

Cowards die many times before their deaths;
The valiant never taste of death but once.
Of all the wonders that I yet have heard,
It seems to me most strange that men should fear;
Seeing that death, a necessary end,
Will come when it will come.

Enter SERVANT.

                 What say the augurers?

    SERVANT.

They would not have you to stir forth to-day.
Plucking the entrails of an offering[2] forth,
They could not find a heart within the beast.

    JULIUS CAESAR.

The gods do this in shame of cowardice:
Cæsar should be a beast without a heart,
If he should stay at home to-day for fear.
No, Cæsar shall not: danger knows full well
That Cæsar is more dangerous than he:[3]
We are two lions litter'd in one day,

---

[1] use: custom.
[2] offering: sacrifice.
[3] **Caesar is more dangerous than he:** Caesar has contempt for danger.

And I the elder and more terrible:—
And Cæsar shall go forth.

CALPHURNIA.

                    Alas, my lord,
Your wisdom is consumed [1] in confidence.
Do not go forth to-day: call it my fear
That keeps you in the house, and not your own.
We'll send Mark Antony to the senate-house;
And he shall say you are not well to-day:
Let me, upon my knee, prevail in this.

JULIUS CAESAR.

Mark Antony shall say I am not well;
And, for thy humour,[2] I will stay at home.

Enter DECIUS.

Here's Decius Brutus, he shall tell them so.

DECIUS BRUTUS.

Cæsar, all hail! good morrow, worthy Cæsar:
I come to fetch you to the senate-house.

JULIUS CAESAR.

And you are come in very happy time,[3]
To bear my greeting to the senators,
And tell them that I will not come to-day:
Cannot, is false; and that I dare not, falser:
I will not come to-day,—tell them so, Decius.

CALPHURNIA.

Say he is sick.

JULIUS CAESAR.

               Shall Cæsar send a lie?
Have I in conquest stretcht mine arm so far
To be afeard to tell graybeards the truth?
Decius, go tell them Cæsar will not come.

---

[1] consumed: lost.
[2] humour: whim.
[3] in very happy time: very appropriate.

DECIUS BRUTUS.

Most mighty Cæsar, let me know some cause,
Lest I be laught at when I tell them so.

JULIUS CAESAR.

The cause is in my will,—I will not come;
That is enough to satisfy the senate.
But, for your private satisfaction,
Because I love you, I will let you know,—
Calphurnia here, my wife, stays[1] me at home:
She dreamt to-night she saw my statua,[2]
Which, like a fountain with an hundred spouts,
Did run pure blood; and many lusty Romans
Came smiling, and did bathe their hands in it:
And these does she apply for warnings and portents
And evils imminent; and on her knee
Hath begg'd that I will stay at home to-day.

DECIUS BRUTUS.

This dream is all amiss interpreted;[3]
It was a vision fair and fortunate:
Your statue spouting blood in many pipes,
In which so many smiling Romans bathed,
Signifies that from you great Rome shall suck
Reviving blood; and that great men shall press
For tinctures, stains, relics, and recognizance.
This by Calphurnia's dream is signified.

JULIUS CAESAR.

And this way have you well expounded it.

DECIUS BRUTUS.

I have, when you have heard what I can say:
And know it now,—the senate have concluded
To give, this day, a crown to mighty Cæsar.

---

[1] stays: detains; keeps.
[2] statua: statue.
[3] amiss interpreted: misinterpreted.

If you shall send them word you will not come,
Their minds may change. Besides, it were a mock[1]
Apt to be render'd,[2] for some one to say,
'Break up the senate till another time,
When Cæsar's wife shall meet with better dreams.'
If Cæsar hide himself, shall they not whisper,
'Lo, Cæsar is afraid'?
Pardon me, Cæsar; for my dear dear love
To your proceeding[3] bids me tell you this;
And reason to my love is liable.[4]

     JULIUS CAESAR.

How foolish do your fears seem now, Calphurnia!
I am ashamed I did yield to them.—
Give me my robe, for I will go:—

    Enter PUBLIUS, BRUTUS, LIGARIUS, METELLUS, CASCA,
            TREBONIUS, *and* CINNA.

And look where Publius is come to fetch me.

     PUBLIUS.

Good morrow, Cæsar.

     JULIUS CAESAR.

                Welcome, Publius.—
What, Brutus, are you stirr'd so early too?—
Good morrow, Casca.—Caius Ligarius,
Cæsar was ne'er so much your enemy
As that same ague[5] which hath made you lean.—
What is't o'clock?

     DECIUS BRUTUS.

             Cæsar, 'tis strucken eight.

---

[1] mock: taunt.
[2] Apt to be render'd: likely to be given in reply.
[3] proceeding: advancement; course of conduct.
[4] reason to my love is liable: it is my love for you that makes me speak in this way.
[5] ague: a sickness characterized by spells of shaking and shivering.

JULIUS CAESAR.

I thank you for your pains and courtesy.

Enter ANTONY.

See! Antony, that revels long o' nights,
Is notwithstanding up.—Good morrow, Antony.

MARCUS ANTONIUS.

So to most noble Cæsar.

JULIUS CAESAR.

                Bid them prepare within:—
I am to blame to be thus waited for.—
Now, Cinna:—now, Metellus:—what, Trebonius!
I have an hour's talk in store for you;
Remember that you call on me to-day:
Be near me, that I may remember you.

TREBONIUS.

Cæsar, I will:—[*aside*] and so near will I be,
That your best friends shall wish I had been further.

JULIUS CAESAR.

Good friends, go in, and taste some wine with me;
And we, like friends, will straightway go together.

DECIUS BRUTUS [*aside*].

That every like is not the same,[1] O Cæsar,
The heart of Brutus yearns to think upon!   [*Exeunt.*

SCENE III.

The same. A street near the Capitol.

Enter ARTEMIDORUS, *reading a paper.*

ARTEMIDORUS.

'Cæsar, beware of Brutus; take heed of Cassius; come not near

---

[1] **every like is not the same:** things that look alike are not always the same; i.e., some people who seem like friends are not friends.

Casca; have an eye to Cinna; trust not Trebonius; mark well
Metellus Cimber; Decius Brutus loves thee not: thou hast
wrong'd Caius Ligarius. There is but one mind in all these
men, and it is bent[1] against Cæsar. If thou beest not immortal, look about you: security gives way to conspiracy.[2]
The mighty gods defend thee! Thy lover,

                          ARTEMIDORUS.'

Here will I stand till Cæsar pass along,
And as a suitor will I give him this.
My heart laments that virtue cannot live
Out of the teeth of emulation.[3]
If thou read this, O Cæsar, thou mayst live;
If not, the Fates[4] with traitors do contrive.[5]   [*Exit.*

SCENE IV.

*The same. Another part of the same street, before
the house of* BRUTUS.

Enter PORTIA *and* LUCIUS.

PORTIA.

I prithee, boy, run to the senate-house;
Stay not to answer me, but get thee gone:
Why dost thou stay?

LUCIUS.

                    To know my errand, madam.

PORTIA.

I would have had thee there, and here again,
Ere I can tell thee what thou shouldst do there.—
[*aside*] O constancy,[6] be strong upon my side,
Set a huge mountain 'tween my heart and tongue!

---

[1] **bent**: directed. [2] **security gives way to conspiracy**: overconfidence
leaves open the way for plots against you. [3] **emulation**: envy;
jealous rivalry. [4] **the Fates**: the three goddesses in Mythology who
controlled human destiny. [5] **contrive**: conspire; plot. [6] **constancy**:
patience; fortitude.

I have a man's mind, but a woman's might.[1]
How hard it is for women to keep counsel! [2]—
Art thou here yet?

LUCIUS.

                Madam, what should I do?
Run to the Capitol, and nothing else?
And so return to you, and nothing else?

PORTIA.

Yes, bring me word, boy, if thy lord look well,
For he went sickly forth: and take good note
What Cæsar doth, what suitors press to[3] him.
Hark, boy! what noise is that?

LUCIUS.

I hear none, madam.

PORTIA.

                Prithee, listen well:
I heard a bustling rumour,[4] like a fray,
And the wind brings it from the Capitol.

LUCIUS.

Sooth,[5] madam, I hear nothing.

Enter the SOOTHSAYER.

PORTIA.

Come hither, fellow: which way hast thou been?

SOOTHSAYER.

At mine own house, good lady.

PORTIA.

What is't o'clock?

SOOTHSAYER.

                About the ninth hour, lady.

PORTIA.

Is Cæsar yet gone to the Capitol?

---

[1] woman's might: woman's strength; hence, weakness.
[2] counsel: a secret.
[3] press to: crowd close to.
[4] bustling rumour: loud clamor; noise of tumult.
[5] Sooth: in truth.

SOOTHSAYER.

Madam, not yet: I go to take my stand,
To see him pass on to the Capitol.

PORTIA.

Thou hast some suit[1] to Cæsar, hast thou not?

SOOTHSAYER.

That I have, lady: if it will please Cæsar
To be so good to Cæsar as to hear me,
I shall beseech him to befriend [2] himself.

PORTIA.

Why, know'st thou any harm's intended towards him?

SOOTHSAYER.

None that I know will be, much that I fear may chance.
Good morrow to you.—Here the street is narrow:
The throng that follows Cæsar at the heels,
Of senators, of prætors,[3] common suitors,
Will crowd a feeble man almost to death:
I'll get me to a place more void, and there
Speak to great Cæsar as he comes along.   [*Exit.*

PORTIA.

I must go in.—[*Aside*] Ay me, how weak a thing
The heart of woman is! O Brutus,
The heavens speed thee in thine enterprise!—
Sure, the boy heard me.—Brutus hath a suit
That Cæsar will not grant.—O, I grow faint.—
Run, Lucius, and commend me to my lord;
Say I am merry:[4] come to me again,
And bring me word what he doth say to thee.

                                   [*Exeunt severally.*

---

[1] suit: message; petition.
[2] befriend: guard.
[3] praetors: magistrates.
[4] merry: in good cheer.

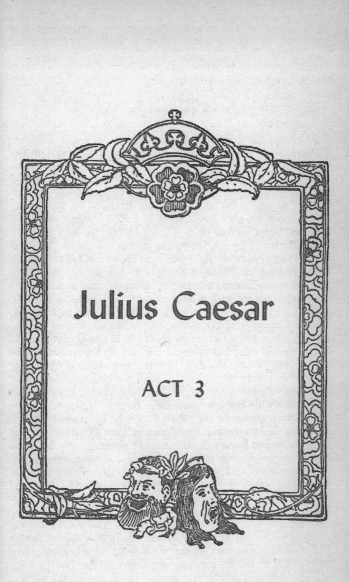

Julius Caesar

ACT 3

ACT III

CAESAR mocks the soothsayer for his earlier prophecy that the ides of March would bring danger to him; but the ides are not yet gone. The written warning is imperiously disregarded for affairs of state; the conspirators gather closely about Caesar, pleading the revocation of a banishment. Caesar becomes more haughty in his refusals and is brought down by daggers. Casca strikes from behind, but Brutus is recognized in his treachery by Caesar in the moment of death. There is a threat of confusion but Brutus summons his followers to a ritual bathing of hands in the blood of a tyrant; then they will issue proclamations as to the justice of their act. Antony's messenger arrives with a discreetly worded plea, and having been given assurances by Brutus of safe conduct (much against Cassius' wishes), Antony himself soon comes. Antony is deeply moved by the brutal spectacle of the corpse and the blood-stained arms but must use all his wits to survive himself and avenge his master later. Brutus allows himself to be prevailed upon, permits Antony to claim the body and to deliver a funeral oration after Brutus has explained the issues and *his* conduct to the confused mob outside. Antony remains with Caesar's body as the others leave; he can vent his genuine grief and rage; and word arrives that Octavius and his army is at hand for aid. The second scene of this act—the two orations—is the pivot of the play. Brutus defends his actions simply and with dignity, and the plebeians seem thoroughly satisfied with the explanations offered and would even refuse Antony speech. It is Brutus's fairness and compassion that is his undoing; he secures attention for Antony and leaves—and the forum is Antony's. Now no longer the easily disregarded "gamesome" attendant of Caesar, Antony plays on the emotions of the mob with superb rhetoric, to the point of mutinying the city against the conspirators. Caesar's legacies to the city arouse the furies of the mob, a foretaste of the civil strife to come. A poet, unhappily named Cinna, becomes a handy substitute for Cinna the conspirator to plebeians out to avenge the wrongs done to Caesar. The conspirators themselves have fled and their houses burn.

ACT III. Scene I.

Rome. Before the Capitol; the SENATE *sitting.*

A crowd of people; among them ARTEMIDORUS *and the* SOOTHSAYER. *Flourish. Enter* CAESAR, BRUTUS, CASSIUS, CASCA, DECIUS, METELLUS, TREBONIUS, CINNA, ANTONY, LEPIDUS, POPILIUS, PUBLIUS, *and others.*

JULIUS CAESAR.
The ides of March are come.
SOOTHSAYER.
Ay, Cæsar; but not gone.
ARTEMIDORUS.
Hail, Cæsar! read this schedule.[1]
DECIUS BRUTUS.
Trebonius doth desire you to o'er-read,
At your best leisure,[2] this his humble suit.
ARTEMIDORUS.
O Cæsar, read mine first; for mine's a suit
That touches Cæsar nearer;[3] read it, great Cæsar.
JULIUS CAESAR.
What touches us ourself, shall be last served.
ARTEMIDORUS.
Delay not, Cæsar; read it instantly.

---

[1] schedule: document; note.
[2] best leisure: most convenient time.
[3] touches Caesar nearer: more important to Caesar.

JULIUS CAESAR.

What, is the fellow mad?

PUBLIUS.

                Sirrah, give place.

CASSIUS.

What, urge you your petitions in the street?
Come to the Capitol.

*CAESAR enters the Capitol, the rest following.
All the SENATORS rise.*

POPILIUS LENA.

I wish your enterprise to-day may thrive.

CASSIUS.

What enterprise, Popilius?

POPILIUS LENA.

              Fare you well. [*Advances to CAESAR.*

MARCUS BRUTUS.

What said Popilius Lena?

CASSIUS.

He wisht to-day our enterprise might thrive.
I fear our purpose is discovered.

MARCUS BRUTUS.

Look, how he makes to[1] Cæsar: mark him.

CASSIUS.

                    Casca,

Be sudden,[2] for we fear prevention.—
Brutus, what shall be done? If this be known,
Cassius or Cæsar never shall turn back,
For I will slay myself.

MARCUS BRUTUS.

             Cassius, be constant:[3]

Popilius Lena speaks not of our purpose;
For, look, he smiles, and Cæsar doth not change.

---

[1] makes to: presses toward.
[2] sudden: alert; quick.
[3] constant: firm.

CASSIUS.

Trebonius knows his time; for, look you, Brutus,
He draws Mark Antony out of the way.

[*Exeunt* ANTONY *and* TREBONIUS. CAESAR *and the* SENATORS
take their seats.

DECIUS BRUTUS.

Where is Metellus Cimber? Let him go,
And presently prefer his suit to Cæsar.

MARCUS BRUTUS.

He is addrest:[1] press near and second him.

CINNA.

Casca, you are the first that rears your hand.

JULIUS CAESAR.

Are we all ready? What is now amiss
That Cæsar and his senate must redress?

METELLUS CIMBER.

Most high, most mighty, and most puissant Cæsar,
Metellus Cimber throws before thy seat
An humble heart,—   [*Kneeling.*

JULIUS CAESAR.

                    I must prevent thee, Cimber.
These couchings[2] and these lowly courtesies
Might fire the blood of ordinary men,
And turn pre-ordinance and first decree
Into the law of children.[3] Be not fond,[4]
To think that Cæsar bears such rebel blood [5]
That will be thaw'd from the true quality
With that which melteth fools; I mean, sweet words,
Low-crooked curt'sies, and base spaniel-fawning.

---

[1] addrest: ready. [2] couchings: stoopings; bows. [3] pre-ordinance and first decree/ Into the law of children: what has been previously ordained and decreed is now of no account; i.e., as stable as the whims of children. [4] fond: foolish. [5] bears such rebel blood: has impulses alien to his usual reasoned judgment.

Thy brother by decree is banished:
If thou dost bend, and pray, and fawn for him,
I spurn thee like a cur out of my way.
Know, Cæsar doth not wrong; nor without cause
Will he be satisfied.

METELLUS CIMBER.

Is there no voice more worthy than my own,
To sound more sweetly in great Cæsar's ear
For the repealing of my banisht brother?

MARCUS BRUTUS.

I kiss thy hand, but not in flattery, Cæsar;
Desiring thee that Publius Cimber may
Have an immediate freedom of repeal.

JULIUS CAESAR.

What, Brutus!

CASSIUS.

　　　　Pardon, Cæsar; Cæsar, pardon:
As low as to thy foot doth Cassius fall,
To beg enfranchisement for Publius Cimber.

JULIUS CAESAR.

I could be well moved, if I were as you;
If I could pray to move, prayers would move me:
But I am constant as the northern star,
Of whose true-fixt and resting[1] quality
There is no fellow[2] in the firmament.
The skies are painted with unnumber'd sparks,[3]
They are all fire, and every one doth shine;
But there's but one in all doth hold his place:
So in the world,—'tis furnisht[4] well with men,
And men are flesh and blood, and apprehensive;
Yet in the number I do know but one
That unassailable holds on his rank,[5]

---

[1] resting: not subject to motion.
[2] fellow: equal.
[3] sparks: stars.
[4] furnisht: provided.
[5] holds on his rank: stays on his course.

Unshaked of motion:[1] and that I am he,
Let me a little show it, even in this,—
That I was constant Cimber should be banisht,
And constant do remain to keep him so.

CINNA.

O Cæsar,—

JULIUS CAESAR.

      Hence! wilt thou lift up Olympus?[2]

DECIUS BRUTUS.

Great Cæsar,—

JULIUS CAESAR.

      Doth not Brutus bootless[3] kneel?

CASCA.

Speak, hands, for me!   [*They stab* CAESAR.

JULIUS CAESAR.

Et tu, Brute? [4]—Then fall, Cæsar!   [*Dies.*

CINNA.

Liberty! Freedom! Tyranny is dead!—
Run hence, proclaim, cry it about the streets.

CASSIUS.

Some to the common pulpits, and cry out,
'Liberty, freedom, and enfranchisement!'

MARCUS BRUTUS.

People, and senators, be not affrighted;
Fly not; stand still:—ambition's debt is paid.

CASCA.

Go to the pulpit, Brutus.

DECIUS BRUTUS.

      And Cassius too.

MARCUS BRUTUS.

Where's Publius?

---

[1] **Unshaked of motion:** immovable resolve.
[2] **wilt thou lift up Olympus?:** will you attempt the impossible?; Mount Olympus in Thessaly was thought to be the abode of the chief gods of ancient Greece.
[3] **bootless:** uselessly; without avail.
[4] *Et tu, Brute?*: And you, too, Brutus?

CINNA.

Here, quite confounded with this mutiny.

METELLUS CIMBER.

Stand fast together, lest some friend of Cæsar's
Should chance—

MARCUS BRUTUS.

Talk not of standing.—Publius, good cheer;
There is no harm intended to your person,
Nor to no Roman else: so tell them, Publius.

CASSIUS.

And leave us, Publius; lest that the people,
Rushing on us, should do your age some mischief.[1]

MARCUS BRUTUS.

Do so:—and let no man abide[2] this deed,
But we the doers.

Enter TREBONIUS.

CASSIUS.

Where is Antony?

TREBONIUS.

                 Fled to his house amazed:
Men, wives, and children stare, cry out, and run
As it were doomsday.

MARCUS BRUTUS.

                     Fates, we will know your pleasures:—
That we shall die, we know; 'tis but the time,
And drawing days out, that men stand upon.[3]

CASSIUS.

Why, he that cuts off twenty years of life
Cuts off so many years of fearing death.

MARCUS BRUTUS.

Grant that, and then is death a benefit:
So are we Cæsar's friends, that have abridged [4]

---

[1] mischief: harm.
[2] abide: answer for; suffer for.
[3] stand upon: trouble about.
[4] abridged: reduced.

His time of fearing death.—Stoop, Romans, stoop,
And let us bathe our hands in Cæsar's blood
Up to the elbows, and besmear our swords:
Then walk we forth, even to the market-place,
And, waving our red weapons o'er our heads,
Let's all cry, 'Peace, freedom, and liberty!'

      CASSIUS.

Stoop then, and wash.—How many ages hence
Shall this our lofty scene be acted over
In states unborn and accents[1] yet unknown!

      MARCUS BRUTUS.

How many times shall Cæsar bleed in sport,[2]
That now on Pompey's basis[3] lies along
No worthier than the dust!

      CASSIUS.

                So oft as that shall be,
So often shall the knot[4] of us be call'd
The men that gave their country liberty.

      DECIUS BRUTUS.

What, shall we forth?

      CASSIUS.

            Ay, every man away:
Brutus shall lead; and we will grace[5] his heels
With the most boldest and best hearts of Rome.

      MARCUS BRUTUS.

Soft! who comes here!

Enter a SERVANT.

A friend of Antony's.

      SERVANT.

Thus, Brutus, did my master bid me kneel;
Thus did Mark Antony bid me fall down;

---

[1] accents: languages; tongues.
[2] sport: performances; plays.
[3] Pompey's basis: base of Pompey's statue.
[4] knot: clique; group.
[5] grace: honor; respect.

And, being prostrate, thus he bade me say:—
Brutus is noble, wise, valiant, and honest;
Cæsar was mighty, bold, royal, and loving:
Say I love Brutus, and I honour him;
Say I fear'd Cæsar, honour'd him, and loved him.
If Brutus will vouchsafe[1] that Antony
May safely come to him, and be resolved [2]
How Cæsar hath deserved to lie in death,
Mark Antony shall not love Cæsar dead
So well as Brutus living; but will follow
The fortunes and affairs of noble Brutus
Thorough[3] the hazards of this untrod state[4]
With all true faith. So says my master Antony.

    MARCUS BRUTUS.

Thy master is a wise and valiant Roman;
I never thought him worse.
Tell him, so please him come unto this place,
He shall be satisfied; and, by my honour,
Depart untoucht.

    SERVANT.

          I'll fetch him presently.   [*Exit.*

    MARCUS BRUTUS.

I know that we shall have him well to friend.

    CASSIUS.

I wish we may: but yet have I a mind
That fears him much; and my misgiving still
Falls shrewdly to the purpose.[5]

    MARCUS BRUTUS.

But here comes Antony.

Enter ANTONY.

      Welcome, Mark Antony.

---

[1] **vouchsafe:** guarantee.
[2] **resolved:** satisfied; cleared of doubt.
[3] **Thorough:** through.
[4] **untrod state:** new state.
[5] **my misgiving still/ Falls shrewdly to the purpose:** my instinctive fears are always well-founded.

MARCUS ANTONIUS.

O mighty Cæsar! dost thou lie so low?
Are all thy conquests, glories, triumphs, spoils,
Shrunk to this little measure? Fare thee well.—
I know not, gentlemen, what you intend,
Who else must be let blood, who else is rank:[1]
If I myself, there is no hour so fit
As Cæsar's death's hour: nor no instrument
Of half that worth as those your swords, made rich
With the most noble blood of all this world.
I do beseech ye, if you bear me hard,[2]
Now, whilst your purpled hands do reek and smoke,
Fulfil your pleasure. Live a thousand years,
I shall not find myself so apt[3] to die:
No place will please me so, no mean of death
As here by Cæsar, and by you cut off,
The choice and master spirits of this age.

MARCUS BRUTUS.

O Antony, beg not your death of us.
Though now we must appear bloody and cruel,
As, by our hands and this our present act,
You see we do; yet see you but our hands,
And this the bleeding business they have done:
Our hearts you see not,—they are pitiful;
And pity to the general wrong of Rome—
As fire drives out fire, so pity pity—
Hath done this deed on Cæsar. For your part,
To you our swords have leaden points, Mark Antony,
Our arms no strength of malice; and our hearts,
Of brothers' temper, do receive you in

---

[1] rank: too full of blood.
[2] bear me hard: hold malice against me.
[3] apt: ready.

With all kind love, good thoughts, and reverence.

CASSIUS.

Your voice shall be as strong as any man's
In the disposing of new dignities.[1]

MARCUS BRUTUS.

Only be patient till we have appeased
The multitude, beside themselves with fear,
And then we will deliver[2] you the cause,
Why I, that did love Cæsar when I struck him,
Have thus proceeded.

MARCUS ANTONIUS.

              I doubt not of your wisdom.
Let each man render me his bloody hand:
First, Marcus Brutus, will I shake with you:—
Next, Caius Cassius, do I take your hand;—
Now, Decius Brutus, yours;—now yours, Metellus;
Yours, Cinna;—and, my valiant Casca, yours;—
Though last, not least in love, yours, good Trebonius.
Gentlemen all,—alas, what shall I say?
My credit[3] now stands on such slippery ground,
That one of two bad ways you must conceit[4] me,
Either a coward or a flatterer.—
That I did love thee, Cæsar, O, 'tis true:
If, then, thy spirit look upon us now,
Shall it not grieve thee dearer[5] than thy death,
To see thy Antony making his peace,
Shaking the bloody fingers of thy foes,
Most noble! in the presence of thy corse?[6]
Had I as many eyes as thou hast wounds,
Weeping as fast as they stream forth thy blood,

---

[1] dignities: offices.

[2] deliver: give.

[3] credit: reputation.

[4] conceit: conceive; think of.

[5] dearer: more bitterly.

[6] corse: corpse.

It would become me better than to close
In terms of friendship[1] with thine enemies.
Pardon me, Julius!—Here wast thou bay'd,[2] brave hart;
Here didst thou fall; and here thy hunters stand,
Sign'd [3] in thy spoil, and crimson'd in thy lethe.[4]—
O world, thou wast the forest to this hart;[5]
And this, indeed, O world, the heart of thee.—
How like a deer, strucken by many princes,
Dost thou here lie!

CASSIUS.

Mark Antony,—

MARCUS ANTONIUS.

Pardon me, Caius Cassius:
The enemies of Cæsar shall say this;
Then, in a friend, it is cold modesty.[6]

CASSIUS.

I blame you not for praising Cæsar so;
But what compact mean you to have with us?
Will you be prickt[7] in number of our friends;
Or shall we on, and not depend on you?

MARCUS ANTONIUS.

Therefore I took your hands; but was, indeed,
Sway'd from the point, by looking down on Cæsar.
Friends am I with you all, and love you all;
Upon this hope, that you shall give me reasons
Why and wherein Cæsar was dangerous.

MARCUS BRUTUS.

Or else were this a savage spectacle:
Our reasons are so full of good regard,[8]
That were you, Antony, the son of Cæsar,
You should be satisfied.

---

[1] close/ In terms of friendship: come to friendly agreement. [2] bay'd: driven to bay; trapped. [3] Sign'd: marked; stained. [4] lethe: death. [5] hart: stag; male deer. [6] cold modesty: unfeeling moderation. [7] prickt: recorded; marked on the list. [8] good regard: thoughtful consideration.

MARCUS ANTONIUS.

　　　　　　　　　That's all I seek:
And am moreover suitor[1] that I may
Produce his body to the market-place;
And in the pulpit, as becomes a friend,
Speak in the order[2] of his funeral.

MARCUS BRUTUS.

You shall, Mark Antony.

CASSIUS.

　　　　　　　Brutus, a word with you.
[*aside to* BRUTUS] You know not what you do: do not consent
That Antony speak in his funeral:
Know you how much the people may be moved
By that which he will utter?

MARCUS BRUTUS [*aside to* CASSIUS].

　　　　　　　　　By your pardon;—
I will myself into the pulpit first,
And show the reason of our Cæsar's death:
What Antony shall speak, I will protest
He speaks by leave and by permission;
And that we are contented Cæsar shall
Have all true rites and lawful ceremonies.
It shall advantage more than do us wrong.

CASSIUS [*aside to* MARCUS BRUTUS].

I know not what may fall;[3] I like it not.

MARCUS BRUTUS.

Mark Antony, here, take you Cæsar's body.
You shall not in your funeral speech blame us,
But speak all good you can devise of Cæsar;
And say you do't by our permission;
Else shall you not have any hand at all

---

[1] suitor: petitioner.
[2] order: course.
[3] fall: happen.

About his funeral: and you shall speak
In the same pulpit whereto I am going,
After my speech is ended.

      MARCUS ANTONIUS.

                        Be it so;
I do desire no more.

      MARCUS BRUTUS.

Prepare the body, then, and follow us.

                      [Exeunt all but ANTONY.

      MARCUS ANTONIUS.

O, pardon me, thou bleeding piece of earth,
That I am meek and gentle with these butchers!
Thou art the ruins of the noblest man
That ever lived in the tide of times.
Woe to the hand that shed this costly[1] blood!
Over thy wounds now do I prophesy,—
Which, like dumb[2] mouths, do ope their ruby lips,[3]
To beg the voice and utterance of my tongue,—
A curse shall light upon the limbs of men;
Domestic fury and fierce civil strife
Shall cumber[4] all the parts of Italy;
Blood and destruction shall be so in use,
And dreadful objects so familiar,
That mothers shall but smile when they behold
Their infants quarter'd with the hands of war;
All pity choked with custom of fell [5] deeds:
And Cæsar's spirit, ranging for revenge,
With Ate[6] by his side come hot from hell,
Shall in these confines with a monarch's voice
Cry 'Havoc,' [7] and let slip the dogs of war;
That this foul deed shall smell above the earth
With carrion men, groaning for burial.

---

[1] costly: rich; noble. [2] dumb: silent. [3] ruby lips: bloody lips.
[4] cumber: encumber. [5] fell: cruel; barbarous. [6] Ate: the Greek
goddess of Mischief and Revenge. [7] Cry 'Havoc': in olden times,
the cry that no quarter was to be given the enemy.

Enter OCTAVIUS' SERVANT.

You serve Octavius Cæsar, do you not?
> SERVANT.

I do, Mark Antony.
> MARCUS ANTONIUS.

Cæsar did write for him to come to Rome.
> SERVANT.

He did receive his letters, and is coming;
And bid me say to you by word of mouth—
O Cæsar!—   [*Seeing the body.*
> MARCUS ANTONIUS.

Thy heart is big, get thee apart and weep.
Passion, I see, is catching; for mine eyes,
Seeing those beads of sorrow stand in thine,
Begin to water. Is thy master coming?
> SERVANT.

He lies to-night within seven leagues of Rome.
> MARCUS ANTONIUS.

Post back with speed, and tell him what hath chanced:[1]
Here is a mourning Rome, a dangerous Rome,
No Rome of safety for Octavius yet;
Hie hence, and tell him so. Yet, stay awhile;
Thou shalt not back[2] till I have borne this corse
Into the market-place: there shall I try,
In my oration, how the people take
The cruel issue[3] of these bloody men;
According to the which, thou shalt discourse
To young Octavius of the state of things.
Lend me your hand.   [*Exeunt with* CAESAR's *body.*

---

[1] chanced: happened.
[2] not back: not come back.
[3] issue: deed.

Scene II.

The same. The Forum.

Enter BRUTUS *and* CASSIUS, *and a throng of* CITIZENS.

CITIZENS.

We will be satisfied; let us be satisfied.

MARCUS BRUTUS.

Then follow me, and give me audience, friends.
Cassius, go you into the other street,
And part[1] the numbers.
Those that will hear me speak, let 'em stay here;
Those that will follow Cassius, go with him;
And public reasons shall be rendered
Of Cæsar's death.

FIRST CITIZEN.

                   I will hear Brutus speak.

SECOND CITIZEN.

I will hear Cassius; and compare their reasons,
When severally[2] we hear them rendered.

                [*Exit* CASSIUS, *with some of the* CITIZENS.
                BRUTUS *goes into the pulpit.*

THIRD CITIZEN.

The noble Brutus is ascended: silence!

MARCUS BRUTUS.

Be patient till the last.
Romans, countrymen, and lovers![3] hear me for my cause;
and be silent, that you may hear: believe me for mine honour; and have respect to mine honour, that you may believe:
censure[4] me in your wisdom; and awake your senses, that
you may the better judge. If there be any in this assembly,
any dear friend of Cæsar's, to him I say, that Brutus' love to

---

[1] part: separate.
[2] severally: separately.
[3] lovers: friends.
[4] censure: judge.

Cæsar was no less than his. If, then, that friend demand why Brutus rose against Cæsar, this is my answer,—Not that I loved Cæsar less, but that I loved Rome more. Had you rather Cæsar were living, and die all slaves, than that Cæsar were dead, to live all free men? As Cæsar loved me, I weep for him; as he was fortunate, I rejoice at it; as he was valiant, I honour him: but, as he was ambitious, I slew him. There is tears for his love; joy for his fortune; honour for his valour; and death for his ambition. Who is here so base that would be a bondman? [1] If any, speak; for him have I offended. Who is here so rude that would not be a Roman? If any, speak; for him have I offended. Who is here so vile that will not love his country? If any, speak; for him have I offended. I pause for a reply.

CITIZENS.

None, Brutus, none.

MARCUS BRUTUS.

Then none have I offended. I have done no more to Cæsar than you shall do to Brutus. The question of his death[2] is enroll'd in the Capitol; his glory not extenuated,[3] wherein he was worthy; nor his offences enforced,[4] for which he suffer'd death. Here comes his body, mourn'd by Mark Antony:

Enter ANTONY *with* CAESAR'S *body.*

who, though he had no hand in his death, shall receive the benefit of his dying, a place in the commonwealth; as which of you shall not? With this I depart,—that, as I slew my best lover for the good of Rome, I have the same dagger for my-self, when it shall please my country to need my death.

---

[1] bondman: slave.
[2] The question of his death: the subject of his death.
[3] extenuated: undervalued; detracted from.
[4] enforced: exaggerated.

CITIZENS.

Live, Brutus! live, live!

FIRST CITIZEN.

Bring him with triumph home unto his house.

SECOND CITIZEN.

Give him a statue with his ancestors.

THIRD CITIZEN.

Let him be Cæsar.

FOURTH CITIZEN.

Cæsar's better parts
Shall be crown'd in Brutus.

FIRST CITIZEN.

We'll bring him to his house with shouts and clamours.

MARCUS BRUTUS.

My countrymen,—

SECOND CITIZEN.

Peace, silence! Brutus speaks.

FIRST CITIZEN.

Peace, ho!

MARCUS BRUTUS.

Good countrymen, let me depart alone,
And, for my sake, stay here with Antony:
Do grace[1] to Cæsar's corpse, and grace his speech
Tending to Cæsar's glories; which Mark Antony,
By our permission, is allow'd to make.
I do entreat you, not a man depart,
Save I alone, till Antony have spoke.   [Exit.

FIRST CITIZEN.

Stay, ho! and let us hear Mark Antony.

---

[1] grace: honor; respect.

THIRD CITIZEN.

Let him go up into the public chair;
We'll hear him.—Noble Antony, go up.

MARCUS ANTONIUS.

For Brutus' sake, I am beholding to you.   [*Goes up.*

FOURTH CITIZEN.

What does he say of Brutus?

THIRD CITIZEN.

                He says, for Brutus' sake,
He finds himself beholding to us all.

FOURTH CITIZEN.

'Twere best he speak no harm of Brutus here.

FIRST CITIZEN.

This Cæsar was a tyrant.

THIRD CITIZEN.

              Nay, that's certain:
We are blest that Rome is rid of him.

SECOND CITIZEN.

Peace! let us hear what Antony can say.

MARCUS ANTONIUS.

You gentle Romans,—

CITIZENS.

           Peace, ho! let us hear him.

MARCUS ANTONIUS.

Friends, Romans, countrymen, lend me your ears;
I come to bury Cæsar, not to praise him.
The evil that men do lives after them;
The good is oft interred with their bones;
So let it be with Cæsar. The noble Brutus
Hath told you Cæsar was ambitious:

If it were so, it was a grievous[1] fault;
And grievously hath Cæsar answer'd it.
Here, under leave[2] of Brutus and the rest,—
For Brutus is an honourable man;
So are they all, all honourable men,—
Come I to speak in Cæsar's funeral.
He was my friend, faithful and just to me:
But Brutus says he was ambitious;
And Brutus is an honourable man.
He hath brought many captives home to Rome,
Whose ransom did the general coffers[3] fill:
Did this in Cæsar seem ambitious?
When that the poor have cried, Cæsar hath wept:
Ambition should be made of sterner stuff:
Yet Brutus says he was ambitious;
And Brutus is an honourable man.
You all did see that on the Lupercal
I thrice presented him a kingly crown,
Which he did thrice refuse: was this ambition?
Yet Brutus says he was ambitious;
And, sure, he is an honourable man.
I speak not to disprove what Brutus spoke,
But here I am to speak what I do know.
You all did love him once,—not without cause:
What cause withholds you, then, to mourn for him?
O judgment, thou art fled to brutish beasts,
And men have lost their reason!—Bear with me;
My heart is in the coffin there with Cæsar,
And I must pause till it come back to me.

    FIRST CITIZEN.

Methinks there is much reason in his sayings.

---

[1] grievous: burdensome; hard to bear.
[2] under leave: by permission.
[3] general coffers: the national treasury.

SECOND CITIZEN.

If thou consider rightly of the matter,
Cæsar has had great wrong.

THIRD CITIZEN.

       Has he, masters?
I fear there will a worse come in his place.

FOURTH CITIZEN.

Markt ye his words? He would not take the crown;
Therefore 'tis certain he was not ambitious.

FIRST CITIZEN.

If it be found so, some will dear abide it.[1]

SECOND CITIZEN.

Poor soul! his eyes are red as fire with weeping.

THIRD CITIZEN.

There's not a nobler man in Rome than Antony.

FOURTH CITIZEN.

Now mark him, he begins again to speak.

MARCUS ANTONIUS.

But yesterday the word of Cæsar might
Have stood against the world: now lies he there,
And none so poor to do him reverence.
O masters, if I were disposed to stir
Your hearts and minds to mutiny and rage,
I should do Brutus wrong, and Cassius wrong,
Who, you all know, are honourable men:
I will not do them wrong; I rather choose
To wrong the dead, to wrong myself, and you,
Than I will wrong such honourable men.
But here's a parchment with the seal of Cæsar,—
I found it in his closet,[2]—'tis his will:
Let but the commons hear this testament,—

---

[1] dear abide it: pay a high penalty.
[2] closet: room.

Which, pardon me, I do not mean to read,—
And they would go and kiss dead Cæsar's wounds,
And dip their napkins in his sacred blood;
Yea, beg a hair of him for memory,
And, dying, mention it within their wills,
Bequeathing it, as a rich legacy,
Unto their issue.[1]

FOURTH CITIZEN.

We'll hear the will: read it, Mark Antony.

CITIZENS.

The will, the will! we will hear Cæsar's will.

MARCUS ANTONIUS.

Have patience, gentle friends, I must not read it;
It is not meet[2] you know how Cæsar loved you.
You are not wood, you are not stones, but men;
And, being men, hearing the will of Cæsar,
It will inflame you, it will make you mad:
'Tis good you know not that you are his heirs;
For, if you should, O, what would come of it!

FOURTH CITIZEN.

Read the will: we'll hear it, Antony;
You shall read us the will,—Cæsar's will.

MARCUS ANTONIUS.

Will you be patient? will you stay awhile?
I have o'ershot myself to tell you of it:
I fear I wrong the honourable men
Whose daggers have stabb'd Cæsar; I do fear it.

FOURTH CITIZEN.

They were traitors: honourable men!

CITIZENS.

The will! the testament!

---

[1] issue: offspring; children.
[2] meet: fitting.

SECOND CITIZEN.

They were villains, murderers: the will! read the will.

MARCUS ANTONIUS.

You will compel me, then, to read the will?
Then make a ring about the corpse of Cæsar,
And let me show you him that made the will.
Shall I descend? and will you give me leave?

CITIZENS.

Come down.

SECOND CITIZEN.

Descend.

THIRD CITIZEN.

You shall have leave.   [ANTONY *comes down.*

FOURTH CITIZEN.

A ring; stand round.

FIRST CITIZEN.

Stand from the hearse, stand from the body.

SECOND CITIZEN.

Room for Antony,—most noble Antony.

MARCUS ANTONIUS.

Nay, press not so upon me; stand far off.

CITIZENS.

Stand back; room; bear back.

MARCUS ANTONIUS.

If you have tears, prepare to shed them now.
You all do know this mantle: I remember
The first time ever Cæsar put it on;
'Twas on a summer's evening, in his tent,
That day he overcame the Nervii:[1]—
Look, in this place ran Cassius' dagger through:
See what a rent the envious Casca made:

---

[1] Nervii: a fierce Belgic tribe conquered by Caesar in 57 B.C.

Through this the well-beloved Brutus stabb'd;
And, as he pluckt his cursed steel away,
Mark how the blood of Cæsar follow'd it,
As rushing out of doors, to be resolved
If Brutus so unkindly knockt, or no;
For Brutus, as you know, was Cæsar's angel:
Judge, O you gods, how dearly Cæsar loved him!
This was the most unkindest cut of all;
For when the noble Cæsar saw him stab,
Ingratitude, more strong than traitors' arms,
Quite vanquisht him: then burst his mighty heart;
And, in his mantle muffling up his face,
Even at the base of Pompey's statua,
Which all the while ran blood, great Cæsar fell.
O, what a fall was there, my countrymen!
Then I, and you, and all of us fell down,
Whilst bloody treason flourisht over us.
O, now you weep; and, I perceive, you feel
The dint[1] of pity: these are gracious drops.
Kind souls, what, weep you when you but behold
Our Cæsar's vesture[2] wounded? Look you here,
Here is himself, marr'd, as you see, with traitors.

     FIRST CITIZEN.
O piteous spectacle!

     SECOND CITIZEN.
O noble Cæsar!

     THIRD CITIZEN.
O woeful day!

     FOURTH CITIZEN.
O traitors, villains!

     FIRST CITIZEN.
O most bloody sight!

---

[1] dint: impression.
[2] vesture: garment.

SECOND CITIZEN.

We will be revenged.

CITIZENS.

Revenge,—about,—seek,—burn,—fire,—kill,—
slay—let not a traitor live!

MARCUS ANTONIUS.

Stay, countrymen.

FIRST CITIZEN.

Peace there! hear the noble Antony.

SECOND CITIZEN.

We'll hear him, we'll follow him, we'll die with him.

MARCUS ANTONIUS.

Good friends, sweet friends, let me not stir you up
To such a sudden flood of mutiny.
They that have done this deed are honourable;—
What private griefs[1] they have, alas, I know not,
That made them do it;—they are wise and honourable,
And will, no doubt, with reasons answer you.
I come not, friends, to steal away your hearts:
I am no orator, as Brutus is;
But, as you know me all, a plain blunt man,
That love my friend; and that they know full well
That gave me public leave to speak of him:
For I have neither wit, nor words, nor worth,
Action, nor utterance, nor the power of speech,
To stir men's blood: I only speak right on;
I tell you that which you yourselves do know;
Show you sweet Cæsar's wounds, poor poor dumb mouths,
And bid them speak for me: but were I Brutus,

---

[1] griefs: grievances.

And Brutus Antony, there were an Antony
Would ruffle up your spirits, and put a tongue
In every wound of Cæsar, that should move
The stones of Rome to rise and mutiny.

CITIZENS.

We'll mutiny.

FIRST CITIZEN.

We'll burn the house of Brutus.

THIRD CITIZEN.

Away, then! come, seek the conspirators.

MARCUS ANTONIUS.

Yet hear me, countrymen; yet hear me speak.

CITIZENS.

Peace, ho! hear Antony,—most noble Antony.

MARCUS ANTONIUS.

Why, friends, you go to do you know not what:
Wherein hath Cæsar thus deserved your loves?
Alas, you know not,—I must tell you, then:—
You have forgot the will I told you of.

CITIZENS.

Most true; the will:—let's stay and hear the will.

MARCUS ANTONIUS.

Here is the will, and under Cæsar's seal:—
To every Roman citizen he gives,
To every several man, seventy-five drachmas.[1]

SECOND CITIZEN.

Most noble Cæsar!—we'll revenge his death.

THIRD CITIZEN.

O royal Cæsar!

MARCUS ANTONIUS.

Hear me with patience.

CITIZENS.

Peace, ho!

---

[1] drachmas: Greek coins.

MARCUS ANTONIUS.

Moreover, he hath left you all his walks,
His private arbours, and new-planted orchards,
On this side Tiber; he hath left them you,
And to your heirs for ever,—common pleasures,
To walk abroad, and recreate yourselves.
Here was a Cæsar! when comes such another?

FIRST CITIZEN.

Never, never.—Come, away, away!
We'll burn his body in the holy place,
And with the brands fire the traitors' houses.
Take up the body.

SECOND CITIZEN.

Go fetch fire.

THIRD CITIZEN.

Pluck down benches.

FOURTH CITIZEN.

Pluck down forms, windows, any thing.

                         [*Exeunt* CITIZENS *with the body.*

MARCUS ANTONIUS.

Now let it work:—mischief, thou art afoot,
Take thou what course thou wilt!

Enter SERVANT.

                         How now, fellow!

SERVANT.

Sir, Octavius is already come to Rome.

MARCUS ANTONIUS.

Where is he?

SERVANT.

He and Lepidus are at Cæsar's house.

MARCUS ANTONIUS.

And thither will I straight[1] to visit him:

---

[1] straight: go immediately.

He comes upon a wish. Fortune is merry,
And in this mood will give us any thing.

SERVANT.

I heard him say, Brutus and Cassius
Are rid [1] like madmen through the gates of Rome.

MARCUS ANTONIUS.

Belike[2] they had some notice of the people
How I had moved them. Bring me to Octavius.   [Exeunt.

SCENE III.

The same. A street.

Enter CINNA *the poet, and after him the* CITIZENS.

CINNA.

I dreamt to-night that I did feast with Cæsar,
And things unlucky charge my fantasy:[3]
I have no will [4] to wander forth of doors,
Yet something leads me forth.

FIRST CITIZEN.

What is your name?

SECOND CITIZEN.

Whither are you going?

THIRD CITIZEN.

Where do you dwell?

FOURTH CITIZEN.

Are you a married man or a bachelor?

SECOND CITIZEN.

Answer every man directly.

FIRST CITIZEN.

Ay, and briefly.

FOURTH CITIZEN.

Ay, and wisely.

THIRD CITIZEN.

Ay, and truly, you were best.[5]

---

[1] Are rid: have ridden.
[2] Belike: perhaps.
[3] charge my fantasy: fill my imagination.
[4] will: wish.
[5] you were best: it were best for you.

CINNA.

What is my name? Whither am I going? Where do I dwell?
Am I a married man or a bachelor? Then, to answer every
man directly and briefly, wisely and truly:—wisely I say, I
am a bachelor.

SECOND CITIZEN.

That's as much as to say, they are fools that marry:—you'll
bear me a bang[1] for that, I fear. Proceed; directly.

CINNA.

Directly, I am going to Cæsar's funeral.

FIRST CITIZEN.

As a friend or an enemy?

CINNA.

As a friend.

SECOND CITIZEN.

That matter is answer'd directly.

FOURTH CITIZEN.

For your dwelling,[2]—briefly.

CINNA.

Briefly, I dwell by the Capitol.

THIRD CITIZEN.

Your name, sir, truly.

CINNA.

Truly, my name is Cinna.

FIRST CITIZEN.

Tear him to pieces; he's a conspirator.

CINNA.

I am Cinna the poet, I am Cinna the poet.

FOURTH CITIZEN.

Tear him for his bad verses, tear him for his bad verses.

---

[1] bear me a bang: stand a blow from me.
[2] For your dwelling: where do you live?

CINNA.

I am not Cinna the conspirator.

FOURTH CITIZEN.

Is is no matter, his name's Cinna; pluck but his name out of his heart, and turn him going.

THIRD CITIZEN.

Tear him, tear him! Come, brands, ho! firebrands: to Brutus', to Cassius'; burn all: some to Decius' house, and some to Casca's; some to Ligarius': away, go!   [*Exeunt.*

Julius Caesar

ACT 4

ACT IV

New ambitions begin to emerge from the ruin of Caesar's. The triumvirate of Antony, Octavius, and Lepidus eliminates any danger of close opposition by proscription, drawing up a list of those to be eliminated: the brother of Lepidus and Antony's nephew are included on the growing list. But Antony would gladly see even Lepidus gone, fit as he is only for errands. Octavius straddles the fence politically, especially as there are still dangers to be faced. The conspirators are quarreling, too. When the two armies meet at Sardis, Brutus flings accusations of base conduct at Cassius, taunts him for his hot temper, dismisses his indignant protestations. But it is not simply the idealist's disgust at the venality of his partner. Brutus's deliberate remoteness is that of sorrow, too, at his wife's horrible suicide, distracted in her grief. The two leaders manage to join once again in friendship. But once more Brutus prevails with ultimately unwise counsel. Rather than adopt a strong defensive position, their armies will advance to attack at Philippi. When all is quiet and Brutus's servant and messengers are fallen asleep in his tent, the ghost of Caesar appears as a visitation to Brutus, to warn him they will meet again at Philippi.

ACT IV. Scene I.

Rome. A room in ANTONY's *house.*

ANTONY, OCTAVIUS, *and* LEPIDUS, *seated at a table.*

MARCUS ANTONIUS.
These many, then, shall die; their names are prickt.[1]
OCTAVIUS CAESAR.
Your brother too must die; consent you, Lepidus?
AEMILIUS LEPIDUS.
I do consent,—
OCTAVIUS CAESAR.
             Prick him down, Antony.
AEMILIUS LEPIDUS.
Upon condition Publius shall not live,
Who is your sister's son, Mark Antony.
MARCUS ANTONIUS.
He shall not live; look, with a spot I damn him.
But, Lepidus, go you to Cæsar's house;
Fetch the will hither, and we shall determine
How to cut off some charge[2] in legacies.
AEMILIUS LEPIDUS.
What, shall I find you here?
OCTAVIUS CAESAR.
              Or here, or at
The Capitol.   [*Exit* LEPIDUS.

---

[1] prickt: marked on the list.
[2] cut off some charge: reduce expense by cutting down the sum of the bequests.

MARCUS ANTONIUS.

This is a slight unmeritable man,
Meet[1] to be sent on errands: is it fit,
The threefold world divided, he should stand
One of the three to share it?

OCTAVIUS CAESAR.

                    So you thought him;
And took his voice[2] who should be prickt to die,
In our black[3] sentence and proscription.

MARCUS ANTONIUS.

Octavius, I have seen more days than you:
And though we lay these honours on this man,
To ease ourselves of divers slanderous[4] loads,
He shall but bear them as the ass bears gold,
To groan and sweat under the business,
Either led or driven, as we point the way;
And having brought our treasure where we will,
Then take we down his load, and turn him off,
Like to the empty ass, to shake his ears,
And graze in commons.[5]

OCTAVIUS CAESAR.

                   You may do your will:
But he's a tried and valiant soldier.

MARCUS ANTONIUS.

So is my horse, Octavius; and for that
I do appoint[6] him store of provender:
It is a creature that I teach to fight,
To wind, to stop, to run directly on,—
His corporal motion govern'd by my spirit.
And, in some taste,[7] is Lepidus but so;
He must be taught, and train'd, and bid go forth;—
A barren-spirited fellow; one that feeds
On abject orts[8] and imitations,
Which, out of use and staled by other men,

---

[1] **Meet:** fit. [2] **voice:** advice. [3] **black:** death. [4] **slanderous:** incriminating. [5] **commons:** community pastures. [6] **appoint:** provide. [7] **taste:** way; degree. [8] **orts:** remnants; scraps of food.

Begin his fashion: do not talk of him
But as a property. And now, Octavius,
Listen great things:—Brutus and Cassius
Are levying powers: we must straight make head:[1]
Therefore let our alliance be combined,
Our best friends made, and our best means stretcht out;
And let us presently go sit in council,
How covert[2] matters may be best disclosed,
And open perils surest answered.[3]

     octavius caesar.
Let us do so: for we are at the stake,
And bay'd about[4] with many enemies;
And some that smile have in their hearts, I fear,
Millions of mischiefs.   [*Exeunt.*

Scene II.

Before brutus' *tent, in the camp near Sardis.*

Drum. Enter brutus, lucilius, lucius, *and the* army;
titinius *and* pindarus *meet them.*

     marcus brutus.
Stand, ho!
     lucilius.
Give the word, ho! and stand.
     marcus brutus.
What now, Lucilius! is Cassius near?

---

[1] straight make head: immediately marshal our forces.
[2] covert: secret.
[3] answered: faced; coped with.
[4] bay'd about: surrounded (as dogs with staked bears).

LUCILIUS.

He is at hand; and Pindarus is come
To do you salutation from his master.

MARCUS BRUTUS.

He greets me well.[1]—Your master, Pindarus,
In his own change, or by ill officers,[2]
Hath given me some worthy cause to wish
Things done, undone: but, if he be at hand,
I shall be satisfied.

PINDARUS.

           I do not doubt
But that my noble master will appear
Such as he is, full of regard [3] and honour.

MARCUS BRUTUS.

He is not doubted.—A word, Lucilius;
How he received you, let me be resolved.[4]

LUCILIUS.

With courtesy and with respect enough;
But not with such familiar instances,[5]
Nor with such free and friendly conference,
As he hath used of old.

MARCUS BRUTUS.

          Thou hast described
A hot friend cooling: ever note, Lucilius,
When love begins to sicken and decay,
It useth an enforced ceremony.[6]
There are no tricks in plain and simple faith:
But hollow men, like horses hot[7] at hand,
Make gallant show and promise of their mettle
But when they should endure the bloody spur,
They fall their crests, and, like deceitful jades,
Sink in the trial. Comes his army on?

---

[1] **He greets me well**: I welcome his greeting. [2] **In his own change, or by ill officers**: by some change of disposition on his part toward me, or by the incompetent handling of his orders by insubordinates. [3] **regard**: respect. [4] **resolved**: assured. [5] **familiar instances**: acts of friendship. [6] **enforced ceremony**: unnatural manner. [7] **hot**: fiery; spirited.

LUCILIUS.

They mean this night in Sardis to be quarter'd;
The greater part, the horse in general,[1]
Are come with Cassius.   *[Low march within.*

MARCUS BRUTUS.

              Hark! he is arrived:—
March gently on to meet him.

Enter CASSIUS *and his* POWERS.

CASSIUS.

Stand, ho!

MARCUS BRUTUS.

Stand, ho! Speak the word along.

FIRST SOLDIER.

Stand!

SECOND SOLDIER.

Stand!

THIRD SOLDIER.

Stand!

CASSIUS.

Most noble brother, you have done me wrong.

MARCUS BRUTUS.

Judge me, you gods! wrong I mine enemies?
And if not so, how should I wrong a brother?

CASSIUS.

Brutus, this sober form[2] of yours hides wrongs;
And when you do them—

MARCUS BRUTUS.

              Cassius, be content;[3]
Speak your griefs[4] softly,—I do know you well:—
Before the eyes of both our armies here,
Which should perceive nothing but love from us,
Let us not wrangle: bid them move away;

---

[1] horse in general: cavalry.
[2] sober form: grave bearing.
[3] content: calm.
[4] griefs: grievances.

Then in my tent, Cassius, enlarge[1] your griefs,
And I will give you audience.

CASSIUS.
                              Pindarus,
Bid our commanders lead their charges off
A little from this ground.

MARCUS BRUTUS.
Lucilius, do you the like; and let no man
Come to our tent till we have done[2] our conference.
Let Lucius and Titinius guard our door.   [*Exeunt.*

SCENE III.

Within the tent of BRUTUS.

Enter BRUTUS *and* CASSIUS.

CASSIUS.
That you have wrong'd me doth appear in this:
You have condemn'd and noted [3] Lucius Pella
For taking bribes here of the Sardians;
Wherein my letters, praying on his side,
Because I knew the man, were slighted off.

MARCUS BRUTUS.
You wrong'd yourself to write in such a case.

CASSIUS.
In such a time as this it is not meet
That every nice offence should bear his comment.

MARCUS BRUTUS.
Let me tell you, Cassius, you yourself
Are much condemn'd to have[4] an itching palm;
To sell and mart your offices for gold
To undeservers.

---

[1] enlarge: give vent to.
[2] done: concluded.
[3] noted: stigmatized.
[4] condemn'd to have: accused of having.

CASSIUS.

I an itching palm!
You know that you are Brutus that speaks this,
Or, by the gods, this speech were else your last.

MARCUS BRUTUS.

The name of Cassius honours this corruption,
And chastisement doth therefore hide his head.

CASSIUS.

Chastisement!

MARCUS BRUTUS.

Remember March, the ides of March remember:
Did not great Julius bleed for justice' sake?
What villain toucht his body, that did stab,
And not for justice? What, shall one of us,
That struck the foremost man of all this world
But for supporting robbers, shall we now
Contaminate our fingers with base bribes,
And sell the mighty space of our large honours
For so much trash as may be grasped thus?—
I had rather be a dog, and bay the moon,
Than such a Roman.

CASSIUS.

Brutus, bay not me,[1]—
I'll not endure it: you forget yourself,
To hedge me in; I am a soldier, I,
Older in practice, abler than yourself
To make conditions.

MARCUS BRUTUS.

Go to; you are not, Cassius.

CASSIUS.

I am.

MARCUS BRUTUS.

I say you are not.

---

[1] bay not me: do not bark at me.

CASSIUS.

Urge[1] me no more, I shall forget myself;
Have mind upon your health, tempt me no further.

MARCUS BRUTUS.

Away, slight man!

CASSIUS.

Is't possible?

MARCUS BRUTUS.

　　　　　Hear me, for I will speak.
Must I give way and room to your rash choler?[2]
Shall I be frighted when a madman stares?

CASSIUS.

O ye gods, ye gods! must I endure all this?

MARCUS BRUTUS.

All this! ay, more: fret till your proud heart break;
Go show your slaves how choleric you are,
And make your bondmen tremble. Must I budge?
Must I observe you?[3] must I stand and crouch
Under your testy humour? By the gods,
You shall digest the venom of your spleen,
Though it do split you; for, from this day forth,
I'll use you for my mirth, yea, for my laughter,
When you are waspish.[4]

CASSIUS.

　　　　　Is it come to this?

MARCUS BRUTUS.

You say you are a better soldier:
Let it appear so; make your vaunting[5] true,
And it shall please me well: for mine own part,
I shall be glad to learn of noble men.

CASSIUS.

You wrong me every way; you wrong me, Brutus;

---

[1] Urge: provoke.
[2] choler: anger.
[3] observe you: take notice of you.
[4] waspish: irascible; petulant.
[5] vaunting: boasting.

I said, an elder soldier, not a better:
Did I say 'better'?

MARCUS BRUTUS.

> If you did, I care not.

CASSIUS.

When Cæsar lived he durst[1] not thus have moved [2] me.

MARCUS BRUTUS.

Peace, peace! you durst not so have tempted him.

CASSIUS.

I durst not!

MARCUS BRUTUS.

No.

CASSIUS.

What, durst not tempt him!

MARCUS BRUTUS.

> For your life you durst not.

CASSIUS.

Do not presume too much upon my love;
I may do that I shall be sorry for.

MARCUS BRUTUS.

You have done that you should be sorry for.
There is no terror, Cassius, in your threats;
For I am arm'd so strong in honesty,
That they pass by me as the idle wind,
Which I respect not. I did send to you
For certain sums of gold, which you denied me;—
For I can raise no money by vile means:
By heaven, I had rather coin my heart,
And drop my blood for drachmas, than to wring
From the hard hands of peasants their vile trash
By any indirection;—I did send

---

[1] durst: dared.
[2] moved: provoked.

To you for gold to pay my legions,
Which you denied me: was that done like Cassius?
Should I have answer'd Caius Cassius so?
When Marcus Brutus grows so covetous,
To lock such rascal counters[1] from his friends,
Be ready, gods, with all your thunderbolts;
Dash him to pieces!

CASSIUS.

                I denied you not.

MARCUS BRUTUS.

You did.

CASSIUS.

I did not:—he was but a fool that brought
My answer back.—Brutus hath rived [2] my heart:
A friend should bear his friend's infirmities,
But Brutus makes mine greater than they are.

MARCUS BRUTUS.

I do not, till you practise them on me.

CASSIUS.

You love me not.

MARCUS BRUTUS.

             I do not like your faults.

CASSIUS.

A friendly eye could never see such faults.

MARCUS BRUTUS.

A flatterer's would not, though they do appear
As huge as high Olympus.

CASSIUS.

Come, Antony, and young Octavius, come,
Revenge yourselves alone on Cassius,
For Cassius is a-weary of the world;
Hated by one he loves; braved [3] by his brother;
Checkt[4] like a bondman; all his faults observed,

---

[1] rascal counters: worthless round pieces of metal used in calculations.
[2] rived: split; torn.
[3] braved: challenged.
[4] Checkt: reproved; called down.

Set in a note-book, learn'd, and conn'd by rote,[1]
To cast into my teeth. O, I could weep
My spirit from mine eyes!—There is my dagger,
And here my naked breast; within, a heart
Dearer than Pluto's[2] mine, richer than gold:
If that thou be'st a Roman, take it forth;
I, that denied thee gold, will give my heart:
Strike, as thou didst at Cæsar; for, I know,
When thou didst hate him worst, thou lovedst him better
Than ever thou lovedst Cassius.

    MARCUS BRUTUS.

                    Sheathe your dagger:
Be angry when you will, it shall have scope;[3]
Do what you will, dishonour shall be humour.[4]
O Cassius, you are yoked with a lamb
That carries anger as the flint bears fire;
Who, much enforced, shows a hasty spark,
And straight is cold again.

    CASSIUS.

              Hath Cassius lived
To be but mirth and laughter to his Brutus,
When grief, and blood ill-temper'd, vexeth him?

    MARCUS BRUTUS.

When I spoke that, I was ill-temper'd too.

    CASSIUS.

Do you confess so much? Give me your hand.

    MARCUS BRUTUS.

And my heart too.

    CASSIUS.

        O Brutus,—

    MARCUS BRUTUS.

                What's the matter?

---

[1] conn'd by rote: learned and read by heart.
[2] Pluto: god of the underworld.
[3] have scope: have full play.
[4] dishonour shall be humour: your insults shall be ascribed to bad temper.

CASSIUS.

Have not you love enough to bear with me,
When that rash humour which my mother gave me
Makes me forgetful?

MARCUS BRUTUS.

                        Yes, Cassius; and, from henceforth,
When you are over-earnest[1] with your Brutus,
He'll think your mother chides, and leave you so.

POET [within].

Let me go in to see the generals;
There is some grudge between 'em, 'tis not meet[2]
They be alone.

LUCILIUS [within].

             You shall not come to them.

POET [within].

Nothing but death shall stay me.

Enter POET, *follow'd by* LUCILIUS, TITINIUS, *and* LUCIUS.

CASSIUS.

How now! what's the matter?

POET.

For shame, you generals! what do you mean?
Love, and be friends, as two such men should be;
For I have seen more years, I'm sure, than ye.

CASSIUS.

Ha, ha! how vilely doth this cynic rime!

MARCUS BRUTUS.

Get you hence, sirrah; saucy fellow, hence!

CASSIUS.

Bear with him, Brutus; 'tis his fashion.

MARCUS BRUTUS.

I'll know his humour, when he knows his time:

---

[1] over-earnest: too vehement.
[2] meet: proper.

What should the wars do with these jigging[1] fools?—
Companion, hence!

> CASSIUS.

           Away, away, be gone!   [*Exit* POET.

> MARCUS BRUTUS.

Lucilius and Titinius, bid the commanders
Prepare to lodge their companies to-night.

> CASSIUS.

And come yourselves, and bring Messala with you
Immediately to us.   [*Exeunt* LUCILIUS *and* TITINIUS.

> MARCUS BRUTUS.

           Lucius, a bowl of wine!

> CASSIUS.

I did not think you could have been so angry.

> MARCUS BRUTUS.

O Cassius, I am sick of many griefs.

> CASSIUS.

Of your philosophy you make no use,
If you give place to accidental evils.

> MARCUS BRUTUS.

No man bears sorrow better:—Portia is dead.

> CASSIUS.

Ha! Portia!

> MARCUS BRUTUS.

She is dead.

> CASSIUS.

How scaped I killing when I crost you so?—
O insupportable and touching loss!—
Upon what sickness?

---

[1] **jigging:** rhyming.

MARCUS BRUTUS.

                Impatient of my absence,
And grief that young Octavius with Mark Antony
Have made themselves so strong;—for with her death
That tidings came;—with this she fell distract,[1]
And, her attendants absent, swallow'd fire.[2]

     CASSIUS.

And died so?

     MARCUS BRUTUS.

           Even so.

     CASSIUS.

                O ye immortal gods!

Enter LUCIUS, *with wine and taper.*

     MARCUS BRUTUS.

Speak no more of her.—Give me a bowl of wine.—
In this I bury all unkindness, Cassius.   [*Drinks.*

     CASSIUS.

My heart is thirsty for that noble pledge.—
Fill, Lucius, till the wine o'erswell the cup;
I cannot drink too much of Brutus' love.   [*Drinks.*

     MARCUS BRUTUS.

Come in, Titinius!   [*Exit* LUCIUS.

Enter TITINIUS, *with* MESSALA.

                Welcome, good Messala.—
Now sit we close about this taper here,
And call in question our necessities.[3]

     CASSIUS.

Portia, art thou gone?

     MARCUS BRUTUS.

                No more, I pray you.—

---

[1] distract: distracted.
[2] swallow'd fire: took poison.
[3] call in question our necessities: discuss our needs.

Messala, I have here received letters,
That young Octavius and Mark Antony
Come down upon us with a mighty power,
Bending[1] their expedition toward Philippi.

MESSALA.

Myself have letters of the selfsame tenour.[2]

MARCUS BRUTUS.

With what addition?

MESSALA.

That by proscription and bills of outlawry,[3]
Octavius, Antony, and Lepidus,
Have put to death an hundred senators.

MARCUS BRUTUS.

Therein our letters do not well agree;
Mine speak of seventy senators that died
By their proscriptions, Cicero being one.

CASSIUS.

Cicero one!

MESSALA.

        Cicero is dead,
And by that order of proscription.—
Had you your letters from your wife, my lord?

MARCUS BRUTUS.

No, Messala.

MESSALA.

Nor nothing in your letters writ of her?

MARCUS BRUTUS.

Nothing, Messala.

MESSALA.

           That, methinks, is strange.

MARCUS BRUTUS.

Why ask you? hear you aught of her in yours?

MESSALA.

No, my lord.

---

[1] Bending: directing.
[2] tenour: tenor; contents.
[3] bills of outlawry: illegal laws.

MARCUS BRUTUS.

Now, as you are a Roman, tell me true.

MESSALA.

Then like a Roman bear the truth I tell:
For certain she is dead, and by strange manner.

MARCUS BRUTUS.

Why, farewell, Portia.—We must die, Messala:
With meditating that she must die once,
I have the patience to endure it now.

MESSALA.

Even so great men great losses should endure.

CASSIUS.

I have as much of this in art as you,[1]
But yet my nature could not bear it so.

MARCUS BRUTUS.

Well, to our work alive. What do you think
Of marching to Philippi presently?[2]

CASSIUS.

I do not think it good.

MARCUS BRUTUS.

                              Your reason?

CASSIUS.

                                        This it is:—
'Tis better that the enemy seek us:
So shall he waste his means, weary his soldiers,
Doing himself offence;[3] whilst we, lying still,
Are full of rest, defence, and nimbleness.

MARCUS BRUTUS.

Good reasons must, of force, give place to better.
The people 'twixt Philippi and this ground
Do stand but in a forced affection;[4]
For they have grudged us contribution:
The enemy, marching along by them,

---

[1] as much of this in art as you: as much of this capacity as you have.
[2] presently: immediately.
[3] Doing himself offence: doing himself harm.
[4] forced affection: compliance through necessity.

By them shall make a fuller number up,[1]
Come on refresht, new-added, and encouraged;
From which advantage shall we cut him off,
If at Philippi we do face him there,
These people at our back.

    CASSIUS.

                      Hear me, good brother.

    MARCUS BRUTUS.

Under your pardon.[2]—You must note beside,
That we have tried the utmost of our friends,
Our legions are brim-full, our cause is ripe:
The enemy increaseth every day;
We, at the height, are ready to decline.
There is a tide in the affairs of men,
Which, taken at the flood, leads on to fortune;
Omitted, all the voyage of their life
Is bound in shallows and in miseries.
On such a full sea[3] are we now afloat;
And we must take the current[4] when it serves,
Or lose our ventures.

    CASSIUS.

               Then, with your will, go on,
We'll along ourselves, and meet them at Philippi.

    MARCUS BRUTUS.

The deep of night is crept upon our talk,
And nature must obey necessity;
Which we will niggard [5] with a little rest.
There is no more to say?

    CASSIUS.

                 No more. Good night:
Early to-morrow will we rise, and hence.

    MARCUS BRUTUS.

Lucius, my gown!—Farewell, good Messala:—

---

[1] **By them shall make a fuller number up**: add to their army by these recruits.

[2] **Under your pardon**: by your leave, I shall continue.

[3] **full sea**: favorable conditions.

[4] **take the current**: take advantage of these conditions.

[5] **niggard**: supply sparingly.

Good night, Titinius:—noble, noble Cassius,
Good night, and good repose.

CASSIUS.

                 O my dear brother!
This was an ill beginning of the night:
Never come such division 'tween our souls!
Let it not, Brutus.

MARCUS BRUTUS.

              Every thing is well.

CASSIUS.

Good night, my lord.

MARCUS BRUTUS.

             Good night, good brother.

TITINIUS AND MESSALA.

Good night, Lord Brutus.

MARCUS BRUTUS.

            Farewell, every one.
         [*Exeunt* CASSIUS, TITINIUS, *and* MESSALA.

Enter LUCIUS, *with the gown.*

Give me the gown. Where is thy instrument?

LUCIUS.

Here in the tent.

MARCUS BRUTUS.

         What, thou speak'st drowsily?
Poor knave, I blame thee not; thou art o'er-watcht.[1]
Call Claudius and some other of my men;
I'll have them sleep on cushions in my tent.

LUCIUS.

Varro and Claudius!

Enter VARRO *and* CLAUDIUS.

VARRO.

Calls my lord?

---

[1] o'er-watcht: worn out from watching; suffering from lack of sleep.

MARCUS BRUTUS.

I pray you, sirs, lie in my tent and sleep;
It may be I shall raise[1] you by and by
On business to my brother Cassius.

VARRO.

So please you, we will stand and watch[2] your pleasure.

MARCUS BRUTUS.

I will not have it so: lie down, good sirs;
It may be I shall otherwise bethink me.—
Look, Lucius, here's the book I sought for so;
I put it in the pocket of my gown.

> [VARRO *and* CLAUDIUS *lie down.*

LUCIUS.

I was sure your lordship did not give it me.

MARCUS BRUTUS.

Bear with me, good boy, I am much forgetful.
Canst thou hold up thy heavy eyes awhile,
And touch thy instrument a strain or two?

LUCIUS.

Ay, my lord, an't[3] please you.

MARCUS BRUTUS.

> It does, my boy:

I trouble thee too much, but thou art willing.

LUCIUS.

It is my duty, sir.

MARCUS BRUTUS.

I should not urge thy duty past thy might;
I know young bloods look for a time of rest.

LUCIUS.

I have slept, my lord, already.

MARCUS BRUTUS.

It was well done; and thou shalt sleep again;

---

[1] raise: awaken.
[2] stand and watch: stand guard as long as you wish.
[3] an't: if it.

I will not hold thee long: if I do live,
I will be good to thee.   [*Music, and a song.*
This is a sleepy tune:—O murderous slumber,
Lay'st thou thy leaden mace[1] upon my boy,
That plays thee music?—Gentle knave, good night:
I will not do thee so much wrong to wake thee:
If thou dost nod, thou break'st thy instrument;
I'll take it from thee; and, good boy, good night.—
Let me see, let me see;—is not the leaf turn'd down
Where I left reading? Here it is, I think.

Enter the GHOST OF CAESAR.

How ill this taper burns!—Ha! who comes here?
I think it is the weakness of mine eyes
That shapes this monstrous apparition.
It comes upon me.—Art thou any thing?
Art thou some god, some angel, or some devil,
That makest my blood cold, and my hair to stare?[2]
Speak to me what thou art.

GHOST OF CAESAR.
Thy evil spirit, Brutus.

MARCUS BRUTUS.
          Why comest thou?

GHOST OF CAESAR.
To tell thee thou shalt see me at Philippi.

MARCUS BRUTUS.
Well; then I shall see thee again?

GHOST OF CAESAR.
Ay, at Philippi.

MARCUS BRUTUS.
Why, I will see thee at Philippi, then.   [GHOST *vanishes.*

---

[1] mace: a heavy staff or club.
[2] stare: stand on end.

Now I have taken heart thou vanishest:
Ill spirit, I would hold more talk with thee.—
Boy, Lucius!—Varro! Claudius!—Sirs, awake!—
Claudius!

LUCIUS.

The strings, my lord, are false.[1]

MARCUS BRUTUS.

He thinks he still is at his instrument.—
Lucius, awake!

LUCIUS.

My lord?

MARCUS BRUTUS.

Didst thou dream, Lucius, that thou so criedst out?

LUCIUS.

My lord, I do not know that I did cry.

MARCUS BRUTUS.

Yes, that thou didst: didst thou see any thing?

LUCIUS.

Nothing, my lord.

MARCUS BRUTUS.

Sleep again, Lucius.—Sirrah Claudius!—
[to VARRO] Fellow thou, awake!

VARRO.

My lord?

CLAUDIUS.

My lord?

MARCUS BRUTUS.

Why did you so cry out, sirs, in your sleep?

VARRO AND CLAUDIUS.

Did we, my lord?

MARCUS BRUTUS.

                    Ay: saw you any thing?

---

[1] false: out of tune.

VARRO.

No, my lord, I saw nothing.

CLAUDIUS.

                Nor I, my lord.

MARCUS BRUTUS.

Go and commend me to my brother Cassius;
Bid him set on his powers betimes[1] before,
And we will follow.

VARRO AND CLAUDIUS.

              It shall be done, my lord.   [*Exeunt.*

---

[1] betimes: promptly.

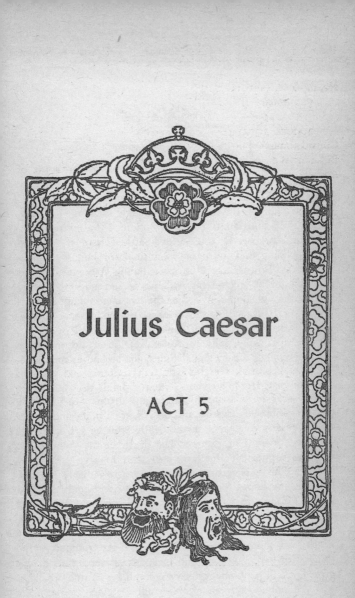

Julius Caesar

ACT 5

ACT V

THE LAST act is a witness to the triumph of the spirit of
Caesar as the two conspirators are inevitably destroyed.
Octavius and Antony watch the enemy armies descend to the
plains at Philippi; the leaders on each side exchange a parley,
trade insults and taunts (the convention of the *flyting*), and
separate to prepare for the decisive battle. Cassius is bothered
by foreboding and, even more unusual for him, by omens
of disaster. Brutus, too, is in a vacillating state; he despises
any thought of suicide but will never surrender to be led
captive through Rome. And thus the two men unhappily part.
The several succeeding scenes chart the collapse of the republican armies; Octavius's flank is overwhelmed by Brutus
but Cassius' army falls to Antony. Disaster occurs when
Cassius wrongly hears that Titinius, his second-in-command,
has been captured, sees his own tents burning and assumes
all to be lost. His bondsman, Pindarus, holds the sword that
slew Caesar for Cassius to fall upon. Brutus discovers the
two dead Romans, Cassius and his officer Titinius, and recog-
nizes Caesar's vengeance in the deaths. But he still has hope
for some reversal of fortune. The death of the young Cato
and the capture of Lucilius, who tries to save Brutus by
posing as his master to the enemy, clearly indicate the collapse of any hopes for Brutus. His army is in confusion and
flight. Turning to a number of friends to hold his sword
steady for him so that he can make a fitting end, he finally
finds Strato to serve him in the task. And he accepts his own
death even more willingly than Caesar's. As trumpets sound
the end of battle, Antony and Octavius arrive to find Brutus
dead but still honored. Antony's epitaph for Brutus proclaims
him the noblest Roman of them all; Octavius prepares for
him the honor of a military funeral.

ACT V. Scene I.

The plains of Philippi.

Enter OCTAVIUS, ANTONY, *and their* ARMY.

OCTAVIUS CAESAR.
Now, Antony, our hopes are answered:
You said the enemy would not come down,
But keep the hills[1] and upper regions:
It proves not so; their battles[2] are at hand;
They mean to warn[3] us at Philippi here,
Answering before we do demand of them.

MARCUS ANTONIUS.
Tut, I am in their bosoms,[4] and I know
Wherefore they do it: they could be content
To visit other places; and come down
With fearful bravery, thinking by this face
To fasten in our thoughts that they have courage;
But 'tis not so.

Enter a MESSENGER.

MESSENGER.
                Prepare you, generals:
The enemy comes on in gallant show;

---

[1] **keep the hills:** stay in the hills.
[2] **battles:** forces.
[3] **warn:** attack.
[4] **in their bosoms:** in their confidence.

Their bloody[1] sign of battle is hung out,
And something to be done immediately.

MARCUS ANTONIUS.

Octavius, lead your battle softly[2] on,
Upon the left hand of the even field.

OCTAVIUS CAESAR.

Upon the right hand I; keep thou the left.

MARCUS ANTONIUS.

Why do you cross me in this exigent?

OCTAVIUS CAESAR.

I do not cross you; but I will do so.   [*March.*

Drum. Enter BRUTUS, CASSIUS, *and their* ARMY; LUCILIUS,
TITINIUS, MESSALA, *and others.*

MARCUS BRUTUS.

They stand, and would have parley.[3]

CASSIUS.

Stand fast, Titinius: we must out and talk.

OCTAVIUS CAESAR.

Mark Antony, shall we give sign of battle?

MARCUS ANTONIUS.

No, Cæsar, we will answer on their charge.
Make forth; the generals would have some words.

OCTAVIUS CAESAR.

Stir not until the signal.

MARCUS BRUTUS.

Words before blows:—is it so, countrymen?

OCTAVIUS CAESAR.

Not that we love words better, as you do.

MARCUS BRUTUS.

Good words are better than bad strokes, Octavius.

---

[1] bloody: red.
[2] softly: slowly.
[3] parley: to confer with an enemy.

MARCUS ANTONIUS.

In your bad strokes, Brutus, you give good words;
Witness the hole you made in Cæsar's heart,
Crying, 'Long live! hail, Cæsar!'

CASSIUS.

                 Antony,
The posture of your blows are yet unknown;
But for your words, they rob the Hybla[1] bees,
And leave them honeyless.

MARCUS ANTONIUS.

                 Not stingless too.

MARCUS BRUTUS.

O, yes, and soundless, too;
For you have stoln their buzzing, Antony,
And very wisely threat before you sting.

MARCUS ANTONIUS.

Villains, you did not so, when your vile daggers
Hackt one another in the sides of Cæsar:
You show'd your teeth like apes, and fawn'd like hounds,
And bow'd like bondmen, kissing Cæsar's feet;
Whilst damned Casca, like a cur, behind
Struck Cæsar on the neck. O you flatterers![2]

CASSIUS.

Flatterers!—Now, Brutus, thank yourself:
This tongue had not offended so to-day,
If Cassius might have ruled.

OCTAVIUS CAESAR.

Come, come, the cause: if arguing make us sweat,
The proof of it[3] will turn to redder drops.
Look,—
I draw a sword against conspirators;
When think you that the sword goes up again?—

---

[1] **Hybla:** a town in Sicily famous for its honey.
[2] **flatterers:** hypocrites.
[3] **proof of it:** result.

Never, till Cæsar's three-and-thirty wounds
Be well avenged; or till another Cæsar
Have added slaughter to the words of traitors.[1]

MARCUS BRUTUS.

Cæsar, thou canst not die by traitors' hands,
Unless thou bring'st them with thee.

OCTAVIUS CAESAR.

                                    So I hope;
I was not born to die on Brutus' sword.

MARCUS BRUTUS.

O, if thou wert the noblest of thy strain,
Young man, thou couldst not die more honourable.

CASSIUS.

A peevish schoolboy, worthless of such honour,
Join'd with a masker and a reveller! [2]

MARCUS ANTONIUS.

Old Cassius still!

OCTAVIUS CAESAR.

                        Come, Antony; away!—
Defiance, traitors, hurl we in your teeth:
If you dare fight to-day, come to the field;
If not, when you have stomachs.[3]

                        [*Exeunt* OCTAVIUS, ANTONY, *and their* ARMY.

CASSIUS.

Why, now, blow wind, swell billow, and swim bark!
The storm is up, and all is on the hazard.

MARCUS BRUTUS.

Ho,
Lucilius! hark; a word with you.

LUCILIUS.

                                    My lord?
                        [BRUTUS *and* LUCILIUS *converse apart.*

---

[1] **Have added slaughter to the words of traitors:** have added another victim because of the words of traitors.

[2] **masker and a reveller:** a masquerader and a rake.

[3] **have stomachs:** are so inclined; have the courage for it.

CASSIUS.

Messala,—

MESSALA.

What says my general?

CASSIUS.

Messala,
This is my birth-day; as this very day
Was Cassius born. Give me thy hand, Messala:
Be thou my witness that, against my will,
As Pompey was, am I compell'd to set[1]
Upon one battle all our liberties.
You know that I held Epicurus strong,[2]
And his opinion: now I change my mind,
And partly credit things that do presage.[3]
Coming from Sardis, on our former[4] ensign
Two mighty eagles fell; and there they percht,
Gorging and feeding from our soldiers' hands;
Who to Philippi here consorted [5] us:
This morning are they fled away and gone;
And in their steads do ravens, crows, and kites,
Fly o'er our heads, and downward look on us,
As we were sickly prey: their shadows seem
A canopy most fatal, under which
Our army lies, ready to give up the ghost.[6]

MESSALA.

Believe not so.

CASSIUS.

I but believe it partly;
For I am fresh[7] of spirit, and resolved
To meet all perils very constantly.[8]

MARCUS BRUTUS.

Even so, Lucilius.

---

[1] set: stake. [2] held Epicurus strong: followed the Epicurean school, which held that the gods scarcely troubled themselves with human affairs. [3] presage: foreshow future events. [4] former: foremost. [5] consorted: accompanied; escorted. [6] give up the ghost: die. [7] fresh: strong. [8] constantly: firmly.

CASSIUS.

               Now, most noble Brutus,
The gods to-day stand friendly, that we may,
Lovers in peace, lead on our days to age!
But, since the affairs of men rest[1] still incertain,
Let's reason with the worst that may befall.
If we do lose this battle, then is this
The very last time we shall speak together:
What are you, then, determined to do?

MARCUS BRUTUS.

Even by the rule of that philosophy
By which I did blame Cato for the death
Which he did give himself:—I know not how,
But I do find it cowardly and vile,
For fear of what might fall,[2] so to prevent
The time of life:—arming myself with patience
To stay[3] the providence of some high powers
That govern us below.

CASSIUS.

               Then, if we lose this battle,
You are contented to be led in triumph
Thorough the streets of Rome?

MARCUS BRUTUS.

No, Cassius, no: think not, thou noble Roman,
That ever Brutus will go bound to Rome;
He bears too great a mind. But this same day
Must end that work the ides of March begun;
And whether we shall meet again I know not.
Therefore our everlasting farewell take:—
For ever, and for ever, farewell, Cassius!
If we do meet again, why, we shall smile;
If not, why, then, this parting was well made.

CASSIUS.

For ever, and for ever; farewell, Brutus!

---

[1] rest: remain.
[2] fall: occur.
[3] stay: await.

If we do meet again, we'll smile indeed;
If not, 'tis true this parting was well made.

MARCUS BRUTUS.

Why, then, lead on.—O, that a man might know
The end of this day's business ere it come!
But it sufficeth that the day will end,
And then the end is known.—Come, ho! away!   [*Exeunt.*

SCENE II.

The same. The field of battle.

Alarums. Enter BRUTUS *and* MESSALA.

MARCUS BRUTUS.

Ride, ride, Messala, ride, and give these bills[1]
Unto the legions on the other side:
Let them set on[2] at once; for I perceive
But cold demeanour[3] in Octavius' wing,
And sudden push gives them the overthrow.
Ride, ride, Messala: let them all come down.   [*Exeunt.*

SCENE III.

The same. Another part of the field.

Alarums.[4] Enter CASSIUS *and* TITINIUS.

CASSIUS.

O look, Titinius, look, the villains fly!
Myself have to mine own turn'd enemy:
This ensign here of mine was turning back;
I slew the coward, and did take it from him.

TITINIUS.

O Cassius, Brutus gave the word too early;
Who, having some advantage on Octavius,
Took it too eagerly: his soldiers fell to spoil,
Whilst we by Antony are all enclosed.[5]

---

[1] bills: messages; written documents.
[2] set on: attack.
[3] cold demeanour: reluctant action.
[4] Alarums: bugle calls signaling action.
[5] enclosed: surrounded.

Enter PINDARUS.

PINDARUS.

Fly further off, my lord, fly further off;
Mark Antony is in your tents, my lord:
Fly, therefore, noble Cassius, fly far off.

CASSIUS.

This hill is far enough.—Look, look, Titinius;
Are those my tents where I perceive the fire?

TITINIUS.

They are, my lord.

CASSIUS.

               Titinius, if thou lovest me,
Mount thou my horse, and hide thy spurs in him,
Till he have brought thee up to yonder troops,
And here again; that I may rest assured
Whether yond troops are friend or enemy.

TITINIUS.

I will be here again, even with a thought.[1]   [*Exit.*

CASSIUS.

Go, Pindarus, get higher on that hill;
My sight was ever thick; regard Titinius,
And tell me what thou notest about the field.—

                       [PINDARUS *goes up.*

This day I breathed first: time is come round,
And where I did begin, there shall I end;
My life is run his compass.[2]—Sirrah, what news?

PINDARUS [*above*].

O my lord!

CASSIUS.

What news?

PINDARUS [*above*].

Titinius is enclosed round about

---

[1] **even with a thought:** quick as a thought.
[2] **compass:** circle; course.

With horsemen, that make to him on the spur;—
Yet he spurs on.—Now they are almost on him;—
Now, Titinius!—
Now some light:¹ O, he lights too: he's ta'en; [*shout*] and,
  hark!
They shout for joy.

  CASSIUS.

                  Come down, behold no more.—
O, coward that I am, to live so long,
To see my best friend ta'en before my face!
    PINDARUS *descends.*
Come hither, sirrah:
In Parthia² did I take thee prisoner;
And then I swore thee, saving of thy life,
That whatsoever I did bid thee do,
Thou shouldst attempt it. Come now, keep thine oath;
Now be a freeman; and, with this good sword,
That ran through Cæsar's bowels, search this bosom.
Stand not to answer: here, take thou the hilts;³
And, when my face is cover'd, as 'tis now,
Guide thou the sword.—Cæsar, thou art revenged,
Even with the sword that kill'd thee.   [*Dies.*
    PINDARUS.
So, I am free; yet would not so have been,
Durst I have done my will. O Cassius!
Far from this country Pindarus shall run,
Where never Roman shall take note of him.   [*Exit.*

          Enter TITINIUS *with* MESSALA.

  MESSALA.
It is but change, Titinius; for Octavius
Is overthrown by noble Brutus' power,

---

¹ **light:** alight; dismount.
² **Parthia:** an ancient country southeast of the Caspian Sea.
³ **hilts:** plural form of hilt (in common usage in Shakespeare's time).

As Cassius' legions are by Antony.

TITINIUS.

These tidings will well comfort Cassius.

MESSALA.

Where did you leave him?

TITINIUS.

                       All disconsolate,
With Pindarus his bondman, on this hill.

MESSALA.

Is not that he that lies upon the ground?

TITINIUS.

He lies not like the living. O my heart!

MESSALA.

Is not that he?

TITINIUS.

                No, this was he, Messala,
But Cassius is no more.—O setting sun,
As in thy red rays thou dost sink to night,
So in his red blood Cassius' day is set,—
The sun of Rome is set! Our day is gone;
Clouds, dews, and dangers come; our deeds are done!
Mistrust[1] of my success hath done this deed.

MESSALA.

Mistrust of good success hath done this deed.
O hateful Error, Melancholy's child,
Why dost thou show to the apt thoughts of men
The things that are not? O Error, soon conceived,
Thou never comest unto a happy birth,
But kill'st the mother that engender'd thee!

TITINIUS.

What, Pindarus! where art thou, Pindarus?

MESSALA.

Seek him, Titinius, whilst I go to meet

---

[1] Mistrust: doubt.

The noble Brutus, thrusting this report
Into his ears: I may say, thrusting it;
For piercing steel, and darts envenomed,
Shall be as welcome to the ears of Brutus
As tidings of this sight.
    TITINIUS.
                Hie you, Messala,
And I will seek for Pindarus the while.   [*Exit* MESSALA.
Why didst thou send me forth, brave Cassius?
Did I not meet thy friends? and did not they
Put on my brows this wreath of victory,
And bid me give it thee? Didst thou not hear their shouts?
Alas, thou hast misconstrued every thing!
But, hold thee, take this garland on thy brow;
Thy Brutus bid me give it thee, and I
Will do his bidding.—Brutus, come apace,
And see how I regarded [1] Caius Cassius.—
By your leave, gods:—this is a Roman's part:
Come, Cassius' sword, and find Titinius' heart.   [*Dies.*

Alarums. Enter MESSALA, *with* BRUTUS, *young* CATO, STRATO,
VOLUMNIUS, *and* LUCILIUS.

    MARCUS BRUTUS.
Where, where, Messala, doth his body lie?
    MESSALA.
Lo, yonder; and Titinius mourning it.
    MARCUS BRUTUS.
Titinius' face is upward.
    YOUNG CATO.
                He is slain.

---

[1] regarded: respected.

MARCUS BRUTUS.

O Julius Cæsar, thou art mighty yet!
Thy spirit walks abroad, and turns our swords
In our own proper entrails.   [*Low alarums.*

YOUNG CATO.

                    Brave Titinius!
Look, whe'r[1] he have not crown'd dead Cassius!

MARCUS BRUTUS.

Are yet two Romans living such as these?—
The last of all the Romans, fare thee well!
It is impossible that ever Rome
Should breed thy fellow.[2]—Friends, I owe more tears
To this dead man than you shall see me pay.—
I shall find time, Cassius, I shall find time.—
Come, therefore, and to Thasos send his body:
His funerals shall not be in our camp,
Lest it discomfort us.—Lucilius, come;—
And come, young Cato;—let us to the field.—
Labeo and Flavius, set our battles on:—
'Tis three o'clock; and, Romans, yet ere night
We shall try fortune in a second fight.   [*Exeunt.*

SCENE IV.

The same. Another part of the field.

Alarum. Enter, fighting, SOLDIERS *of both armies; then* BRUTUS,
YOUNG CATO, LUCILIUS, *and others.*

MARCUS BRUTUS.

Yet, countrymen, O, yet hold up your heads!

YOUNG CATO.

What bastard doth not? Who will go with me?
I will proclaim my name about the field:—

---

[1] whe'r: whether.
[2] fellow: equal.

I am the son of Marcus Cato, ho!
A foe to tyrants, and my country's friend;
I am the son of Marcus Cato, ho!

MARCUS BRUTUS.

And I am Brutus, Marcus Brutus, I;
Brutus, my country's friend; know me for Brutus!   [*Exit.*

LUCILIUS.

O young and noble Cato, art thou down?
Why, now thou diest as bravely as Titinius;
And mayst be honour'd, being Cato's son.

FIRST SOLDIER.

Yield, or thou diest.

LUCILIUS.

Only I yield to die:
There is so much that thou wilt kill me straight;[1]
                                        [*Offering money.*

Kill Brutus, and be honour'd in his death.

FIRST SOLDIER.

We must not.—A noble prisoner!

SECOND SOLDIER.

Room, ho! Tell Antony, Brutus is ta'en.

FIRST SOLDIER.

I'll tell the news:—here comes the general.

                    Enter ANTONY.

Brutus is ta'en, Brutus is ta'en, my lord.

MARCUS ANTONIUS.

Where is he?

LUCILIUS.

Safe, Antony; Brutus is safe enough:
I dare assure thee that no enemy
Shall ever take alive the noble Brutus:
The gods defend him from so great a shame!

---

[1] straight: immediately.

When you do find him, or alive or dead,
He will be found like Brutus, like himself.

    MARCUS ANTONIUS.

This is not Brutus, friend; but, I assure you,
A prize no less in worth: keep this man safe,
Give him all kindness: I had rather have
Such men my friends than enemies. Go on,
And see whe'r Brutus be alive or dead;
And bring us word unto Octavius' tent
How every thing is chanced.[1]   [*Exeunt.*

SCENE V.

The same. Another part of the field.

Enter BRUTUS, DARDANIUS, CLITUS, STRATO, *and* VOLUMNIUS.

    MARCUS BRUTUS.

Come, poor remains of friends,[2] rest on this rock.

    CLITUS.

Statilius show'd the torch-light; but, my lord,
He came not back: he is or ta'en or slain.

    MARCUS BRUTUS.

Sit thee down, Clitus: slaying is the word;
It is a deed in fashion. Hark thee, Clitus.   [*Whispers him.*

    CLITUS.

What, I, my lord? No, not for all the world.

    MARCUS BRUTUS.

Peace, then, no words.

    CLITUS.

            I'll rather kill myself.

---

[1] **chanced**: resolved.
[2] **poor remains of friends**: few remaining friends.

MARCUS BRUTUS.

Hark thee, Dardanius.   [*Whispers him.*

DARDANIUS.

           Shall I do such a deed?

CLITUS.

O Dardanius!

DARDANIUS.

O Clitus!

CLITUS.

What ill request did Brutus make to thee?

DARDANIUS.

To kill him, Clitus. Look, he meditates.

CLITUS.

Now is that noble vessel full of grief,
That it runs over even at his eyes.

MARCUS BRUTUS.

Come hither, good Volumnius; list a word.[1]

VOLUMNIUS.

What says my lord?

MARCUS BRUTUS.

        Why, this, Volumnius:
The ghost of Cæsar hath appear'd to me
Two several times by night,—at Sardis once,
And, this last night, here in Philippi fields:
I know my hour is come.

VOLUMNIUS.

        Not so, my lord.

MARCUS BRUTUS.

Nay, I am sure it is, Volumnius.
Thou seest the world, Volumnius, how it goes;
Our enemies have beat us to the pit:[2]   [*Low alarums.*
It is more worthy to leap in ourselves,
Than tarry[3] till they push us. Good Volumnius,

---

[1] list a word: listen to a word.
[2] pit: grave.
[3] tarry: wait.

Thou know'st that we two went to school together:
Even for that our love of old, I prithee,
Hold thou my sword-hilts, whilst I run on it.

VOLUMNIUS.

That's not an office[1] for a friend, my lord.   [*Alarum still.*

CLITUS.

Fly, fly, my lord; there is no tarrying here.

MARCUS BRUTUS.

Farewell to you;—and you;—and you, Volumnius.—
Strato, thou hast been all this while asleep;
Farewell to thee too, Strato.—Countrymen,
My heart doth joy, that yet, in all my life,
I found no man but he was true to me.
I shall have glory by this losing day,
More than Octavius and Mark Antony
By this vile conquest shall attain unto.
So, fare you well at once; for Brutus' tongue
Hath almost ended his life's history:
Night hangs upon mine eyes; my bones would rest,
That have but labour'd to attain this hour.

                    [*Alarums. Cry within,* 'Fly, fly, fly!'

CLITUS.

Fly, my lord, fly.

MARCUS BRUTUS.

                Hence! I will follow.

            [*Exeunt* CLITUS, DARDANIUS, *and* VOLUMNIUS.

I prithee, Strato, stay thou by the lord:
Thou art a fellow of a good respect;[2]

---

[1] **an office**: a proper action.
[2] **respect**: reputation.

Thy life hath had some smatch[1] of honour in it:
Hold, then, my sword, and turn away thy face,
While I do run upon it. Wilt thou, Strato?

    STRATO.

Give me your hand first: fare you well, my lord.

    MARCUS BRUTUS.

Farewell, good Strato.—Cæsar, now be still:
I kill'd not thee with half so good a will.

                 [*He runs on his sword, and dies.*

    Alarums. Retreat. Enter OCTAVIUS, ANTONY, MESSALA,
            LUCILIUS, *and the* ARMY.

    OCTAVIUS CAESAR.

What man is that?

    MESSALA.

My master's man.—Strato, where is thy master?

    STRATO.

Free from the bondage you are in, Messala:
The conquerors can but make a fire of him;
For Brutus only overcame himself,
And no man else hath honour by his death.

    LUCILIUS.

So Brutus should be found.—I thank thee, Brutus,
That thou hast proved Lucilius' saying true.

    OCTAVIUS CAESAR.

All that served Brutus, I will entertain them[2]—
Fellow, wilt thou bestow thy time with me?

    STRATO.

Ay, if Messala will prefer[3] me to you.

    OCTAVIUS CAESAR.

Do so, good Messala.

    MESSALA.

How died my master, Strato?

---

[1] **smatch:** small amount; smack.
[2] **entertain them:** take them into his service.
[3] **prefer:** recommend.

STRATO.

I held the sword, and he did run on it.

MESSALA.

Octavius, then take him to follow thee,
That did the latest service to my master.

MARCUS ANTONIUS.

This was the noblest Roman of them all:
All the conspirators, save only he,
Did that they did in envy of great Cæsar;
He only, in a general honest thought,
And common good to all, made one of them.
His life was gentle; and the elements
So mixt in him, that Nature might stand up
And say to all the world, 'This was a man!'

OCTAVIUS CAESAR.

According to his virtue let us use[1] him,
With all respect and rites of burial.
Within my tent his bones to-night shall lie,
Most like a soldier, order'd [2] honourably.—
So, call the field to rest: and let's away,
To part[3] the glories of this happy day.   [*Exeunt.*

[1] use: treat.
[2] order'd: prepared for burial.
[3] part: share.